CHARLIE AND ME

CHARLIE AND ME

Charles Manson and the Reporter Who Came to Know the Most Famous Mass Murderer in History

Mary Neiswender
with Kate Neiswender

Potomac Books
An imprint of the University of Nebraska Press

 Potomac Books is an imprint of the University of Nebraska Press.
Manufactured in the United States of America.

For customers in the EU with safety/GPSR concerns, contact:
gpsr@mare-nostrum.co.uk
Mare Nostrum Group BV
Mauritskade 21D
1091 GC Amsterdam
The Netherlands

Library of Congress Cataloging-in-Publication Data
Names: Neiswender, Mary, author. | Neiswender, Kate, author.
Title: Charlie and me: Charles Manson and the reporter who came to know the most famous mass murderer in history / Mary Neiswender with Kate Neiswender.
Description: Lincoln: Potomac Books, an imprint of the University of Nebraska Press, [2025] | Includes index.
Identifiers: LCCN 2025020549
ISBN 9781640126688 (paperback)
ISBN 9781640126855 (epub)
ISBN 9781640126862 (pdf)
Subjects: LCSH: Manson, Charles, 1934–2017. | Murderers—United States. | Criminals—United States.
Classification: LCC HV6248 .M2797 N45 2025
LC record available at https://lccn.loc.gov/2025020549

Designed and set in Arno Pro by Lacey Losh.

To every woman working in a man's world:
Do what you love. It will be okay.

Contents

LIST OF ILLUSTRATIONS ix

PREFACE xi

1. Charlie Manson and Me 1
2. A Little Bit about Me 17
3. Charlie's Girls 23
4. The Family 47
5. Gary Hinman, Shorty Shea, the Symbionese Liberation Army, and More 55
6. The Press Were Part of the Story 63
7. The Defense of Charles Manson 77
8. Prosecuting Charlie and His Girls 93
9. Charlie in His Own Words 115
10. He Never Left the Public Eye 133

INDEX 137

Illustrations

Following page 62

1. Mary Neiswender at the *Press-Telegram*
2. Staff of the *Independent Press-Telegram*
3. Mary Neiswender's Pulitzer Prize nominations
4. Announcement of Mary Neiswender's election as president of the Los Angeles Press Club
5. Mary Neiswender's press credentials
6. Los Angeles Press Club's newsletter featuring Mary Neiswender's accomplishments
7. District attorney's confidential memo regarding Susan Atkins
8. Los Angeles Police Department press release regarding the Tate murders
9. Homicide investigation regarding LaBianca murders
10. Psychological evaluation of Patricia Krenwinkel
11. Spahn Ranch's "Gypsy Shack"
12. Newspaper article featuring "Charlie's girls"
13. The two faces of Charlie Manson
14. Press corps' Helter Skelter party invitation
15. "Hippie Murders" parody song sheet from Helter Skelter party

16. The press corps at Helter Skelter party

17. "Sob Sisters" of the Manson trial

18. Court sketch of Manson's attorney Irving Kanarak

19. Court sketch demonstrating Manson's frustrations with the trial protocols

20. Court sketch of the three defendants—Patricia Krenwinkel, Susan Atkins, and Leslie Van Houten

21. Court sketch of the Manson trial verdict

22. A sketch artist's gift to Mary Neiswender signed by members of the press corps

23. Interview requests for Manson post-trial

24. A Christmas card from Tex Watson

25. Manson's prison letters to Mary Neiswender

Preface

In 1970, reporter Mary Neiswender was covering the trial of accused mass murderer Charles Manson and his bevy of girls. She was one of dozens of other reporters from the United States and around the world.

No one could get to Charlie himself. He was heavily guarded in the Los Angeles County Jail and would not—or could not—speak to any reporters, admirers, or curiosity-seekers.

Through one of Mary's many informants, a longshoreman with a friend in the jail, she managed a quick phone call with Charlie, and that call unlocked a relationship that lasted for the next five decades. Mary spoke to Charlie when no one else could, and he kept talking to her even while her lurid headlines about a "Wolf Pack Gang of Thrill Killers" were pasted on newspapers around the country. Her colorful phrasing became well known, based on her face-to-face interviews with the country's most notorious man. Her stories were picked up by the wire services, *Newsweek*, and other national and international news outlets.

This is the story of Charlie Manson, a man who spent most of his life in institutions before the famous killings, and who died quietly in prison in 2017. He was not insane or a Svengali-like figure, as some have claimed. He was intelligent, well-spoken, and—yes—a killer.

This is the story of Charlie Manson from someone who got to know him perhaps better than anyone else: a reporter.

CHARLIE AND ME

1 Charlie Manson and Me

When I first spoke to Charlie Manson, he was curled up under a table at the law library reserved for inmates of the Los Angeles County Jail. How he got under the table is a big part of the story.

Someone had murdered Sharon Tate and her friends in August 1969, and had murdered Leno and Rosemary LaBianca as well. Charlie was arrested and labeled a cult guru, a monster, who used drugs and orgies to twist his girls into mass murder. No one had talked to Charlie himself, although every reporter in the country wanted to. He was under constant guard, and he was kept away from the telephone. Charlie was in a high security part of the jail, and there were extra guards posted. You couldn't get in unless you were listed by Charlie as a friend or a witness, and even then there were restrictions: if you were a friend, but you had a criminal record, you couldn't get in. And most—if not all—of Charlie's friends had criminal records.

I had been covering "cops and courts" for almost twenty years by then, with a lot of time down at the LA waterfront. I received a call from a friend of mine, a longshoreman. I had done a favor for him once, and he wanted to pay me back. He told me he knew someone who could get me to Manson.

The longshoreman put me in contact with a man who wanted to meet at eleven o'clock at night in a crime-ridden part of the LA harbor. Why, I asked, why Wilmington and why in the middle of the night? He doesn't want to be seen with you, was the answer. I was crazy to go, but I did.

The mystery man said he had a friend in the same area of the jail as Charlie. His friend in jail would call me at the newspaper office, then put Charlie on the phone. Two days later, at the preset time, the phone rang at my desk.

I was worried about my longshoreman friend, and his friend, and even the guy in jail. If anyone ever found out about this, there would be hell to pay. Fifty years later, I am still worried about these guys. I haven't been able to find out if any of them are still alive, although I feel I'm the last man standing.

But when the phone rang, I didn't think about that or anything else, just the possibility of getting the most sought-after interview in the United States—Charlie Manson. Someone, a voice I didn't recognize, said, "Mary? Make it quick." The phone changed hands.

I now had maybe a minute or two to convince Charlie that he should talk to me, not on the phone, but rather in person, face-to-face. I knew he didn't like the "system." He had been in and out of institutions or jail since he was a kid. I also knew he probably wanted to tell his side of the story. He wasn't allowed to speak in his early court appearances and everyone watching could tell it really frustrated him.

After all these years, I can't remember exactly what I said, but I know what I said first.

"Charlie? This is Mary Neiswender."

Charlie interrupted. He knew who I was.

"Yeah. Neil told me about you." Neil was the guy at the table in the law library, friend to the mystery man from Wilmington.

I had Charlie on the phone, and three of my editors were hovering around me, stage-whispering directions, which almost blew the entire thing. During my very delicate conversation with Charlie, these three men were talking at me, disbelieving I had Charles Manson on the phone, and at the same time wanting to take over the call. They would not shut up until I used some choice vulgarities and told them they were about to blow the story.

I told Charlie that I could get his side of the story out. He wanted that, and he wanted it badly enough that he listed me as a "friend" so I could get into the jail and talk to him. I went in the next day.

We spent a couple of hours talking that first time, face-to-face, in the Los Angeles County Jail, in a visitor's room.

He smiled at me.

"So, you're Mary."

I smiled back.

"So, you're Charlie."

Guards were posted every few feet, as if Charlie—all 125 pounds of him—could suddenly bolt and kill everyone in sight. For the next few years, I saw this over and over again. Small and slender Charlie Manson, five feet three inches tall, guarded by big burly sheriff's deputies twice his weight and all muscle. They were scared that Charlie would do something. I'm not sure what, given the circumstances.

What followed were dozens of in-person interviews just inches away from Charlie, separated by two inches of plexiglass. There were many more by phone. I was always amazed when he called.

That first interview was in January 1970. The trial would not begin for another six months, but the public was fascinated with Charlie, his girls, and his gang at the Spahn Ranch. The story was a phenomenon. No other reporter had even gotten close to Charlie. But he was telling me about his defense, his childhood, his girls. Everything. In that first story, published January 31, 1970, Charlie told me he would defend himself in song, not in words.

Charlie told me that his version of the Tate-LaBianca case would be released in a series of records, although he didn't know whether those would be singles or a full album. He said the record companies already had a bunch of his tapes, but he was vague about how he got a tape recorder (the judge had denied that request) and then got the tapes out of the jail. I would later learn that his ability to get things in and out of jail was close to magical. When pressed, he said: "They not only haven't given me a tape recorder, they haven't given me anything. They're taking things away, and now they won't even let me talk to my witnesses—none of them." He added, "Sadie (Susan Atkins) wants to see me, but her attorney won't let her. She's gotten word to me that if I find her a good attorney, she'll shut up."

At this point, Sadie had spilled her story for $200,000, and it contained a lot of detail on how Charlie masterminded the murders. Later, Linda Kasabian would weave a story worthy of a horror movie, all while being told she was immune from prosecution.

In this first face-to-face interview, Charlie was persuasive, soft-spoken. He spoke well and seemed well-educated, although I knew he had never finished school. He was street-smart. In the years to come, I would sometimes have to remind myself that this was one of the world's most famous mass murders, even though he never killed anyone at the Tate or LaBianca houses. He had allegedly killed others, if witnesses were to be believed, but Charlie denied his involvement in any violent acts from the beginning. I knew, in my gut, that he was guilty of murder. But he was still charming.

Charlie told me the judge was severely limiting his ability to speak with witnesses:

> They say I'm my own attorney, so other attorneys can't bring in witnesses. So I told them to just let the witnesses come in alone, but then they say they can't because I've already seen some of them three times, and that's the limit. But I say that's not enough time to work out a case like this.
>
> Some of the people hitch-hike to get here. There were 150 persons—off and on—that lived at that [Spahn] Ranch . . . and like, they're strung all over the country. People are hitch-hiking all over trying to find people that were there during that time. They come in and they talk [with me] for maybe five or ten minutes, and go out looking for someone else.

He explained that the folks that lived on Spahn Ranch were nomads and kept traveling from place to place. He said that finding those people would save him, but he knew it would be tough.

In January 1970, six months before trial, Charlie was obviously frustrated with a system that assumed he was guilty and gave him no ability to talk to witnesses or work up his case. "I've already been tried, convicted and executed in print." I had to cringe at that. I had written about him as well, often and sometimes sensationally. But the interview went on, and he was oddly optimistic. "They've never had a case. I'm supposed to be innocent until proven guilty. I'll let them prove it." Sadly, he said, "Nothing can hurt me more than I'm already hurt."

Charlie tried to convince me that the real murderers were still on the loose:

> Some atrocious murders were perpetrated. So they say, "Well, we've got to find somebody, so we'll take these people here"—meaning us. But the murders are still going on. You know the machine will not admit that it's wrong . . . will not say, "We have got the wrong people . . . the killers are still on the loose." They're covering up the thing as much as they can.
>
> Some friends of mine told me some people were killed in Santa Barbara—after I got in jail—and they're still trying to blame it on me.

Charlie told me the authorities were trying to pin other crimes on him as well. On May 27, 1969, two months before the Tate-LaBianca murders, Charlie's sixty-four-year-old uncle, Darwin "Scotty" Scott, was found dead in his home in Ashland, Kentucky. He had been stabbed nineteen times, and finally pinned to the floor with a butcher knife. Charlie claimed he knew nothing about it, but it would seem that every case involving stab wounds was being examined by the authorities to see if Charlie and his followers had anything to do with it.

Charlie's proposal that he would present his defense musically never panned out. He said that he was on the verge of a record contract at one point, thanks to help from Dennis Wilson of the Beach Boys. It was apparently the Beach Boys angle that led to the Tate killings. The house Roman Polanski leased for himself and Sharon Tate had once been occupied by Terry Melcher, a record producer who had turned down Manson's music. Manson remembered the house, and the jury was told Manson had visited the house in March 1969. By the time of the murders in August 1969, Melcher no longer lived there. Because the murders of Sharon Tate and the others were linked to Melcher, prosecutor Vince Bugliosi brought in Melcher to testify.

Melcher told the jury that he had auditioned Charlie at the Spahn Ranch in May 1969, but wasn't impressed with Charlie's talent. Melcher said he went to the Ranch at the insistence of his then talent scout. The audition was held in a stream bed, with forty of Charlie's girls participating: "Charlie sat on a rock and sang about fifteen songs, and the others were sitting around him. It lasted two to three hours but I wasn't too impressed by the songs. I was more impressed by the whole scene. I was impressed by Charlie's strength and the obvious leadership he had over these people. I was impressed how he could survive out there in the country. It was a totally different way of life."

Melcher described Charlie's singing as "average," and told the jury that even his guitar playing "wasn't as good most people he [Melcher] worked with."

After the audition, Melcher said things turned strange, a common problem at Spahn Ranch: "Randy Starr is a Hollywood stuntman and he had a six-gun strapped to his waist. I don't know if it was loaded, but Randy was going to draw on somebody and Charlie intervened—I think he hit him in the stomach. I'm glad he did." Melcher never saw Charlie again.

Charlie's album did get issued in 1970, and you can still listen to it online. The music industry wouldn't touch it, but the Family got together and paid for its release. The Family chose one of the most wild-eyed crazy-cult-leader photos they could find for the front, and called the album *Lie,* faking the cover of *Life* magazine without the *f*. I'm no music critic, but it sounded like much of the music coming out at the time. He might have been successful with it if given a chance . . . and if he hadn't become the most notorious criminal in American history.

Over the next year, Charlie and I met a number of times. He and I spoke on the phone frequently, both at the office and at home. Unfortunately, he also sent some of his Family to my house, to let me know he knew where I lived. He shifted between being gentle and intelligent to being aggressive and nearly mad; he changed on a dime, and I believe most of the time, he was doing it intentionally, to make a point. For example, I pushed him to talk about his life, his childhood, his biological family. He went into what I labeled his "you are me and I am you and we are us" routine. At first, I would bring him back to the real world slowly, gingerly. Later, I got bolder.

I noticed how carefully he would watch my face to see how far he could push me. When he felt he had gone over the line, he would break into his little-kid smile. He knew what he was doing, at least that's the way it seemed to me. The Svengali label that some put on him, calling Charlie crazy, I didn't see that. Was he evil? I don't think so. I am certain he did some very bad things, including murder. But there was humanity in him. I know the difference. I have interviewed many mass murderers, and I can think of some—the Freeway Killer, Bill Bonin, comes to mind—who were pure evil, with a kind of presence that made me want to walk out of the jail and go to church. But not Charlie. He wasn't like that.

He had an infectious smile which put you at ease, leading you to think he could do no wrong. Cellmates, police officers, and even judges who came into close contact with him admitted he really seemed like a nice guy.

And Charlie was the first to agree with them.

In the early stages of the case, reporters who saw him and listened to him speak would say of Charlie's guilt, "I just don't know." That was, until they saw his background, the years in juvenile facilities, jails, and prisons, and then they leaned toward guilt.

Charlie's first face-to-face interview with me was a test. I think he wanted to know if I thought he was guilty, although he never asked. He talked about how he was writing songs for his defense, and that his case would be in music. I wrote about that, but he never mentioned it again. He was, I'm sure, checking to see if I would buy his story. I know he read my paper.

He also said that Sadie Atkins was going to recant her testimony, which was much more important. Susan "Sadie" Atkins, only twenty-one years old, had testified in front of the Los Angeles County Grand Jury in December 1969, and had implicated Charlie, Linda Kasabian, Patricia Krenwinkel, Charles "Tex" Watson, and Leslie Van Houten. The Grand Jury deliberated only twenty minutes before bringing back the indictments. Sadie had testified in front of the Grand Jury for more than two hours and provided the bloody details of both the Sharon Tate killings and the murders of Leno and Rosemary LaBianca, who were killed the next day.

I went back to talk to Charlie again, and quickly, after our first meeting. This interview was more serious, and he again talked about Sadie Atkins's testimony, this time insisting that none of the others would back up Sadie's story: "None of them will talk like Sadie because there's really nothing to talk about." Charlie never admitted killing anyone, although he knew a great many details that no one else apparently knew.

"I've got thirty witnesses all on my side, all willing to testify that I didn't go around killing people." He smiled at me. "I'm too small to be violent. I weigh 125 pounds, and I learned a long time ago to keep my mouth shut and stay in my place."

It's true that none of the witnesses could place Charlie at the site of either of the murders, not at the Tate house, nor at the LaBiancas'. It's true that Charlie was a small man. He was only five-foot-three and slender, but his strength lay in his power of persuasion. He may not have been present at the murders, but the witnesses—first Sadie Atkins, and later Linda Kasabian—swore that he had told them where to go, when to go, and how to kill.

While Charlie was in jail, his girls—his Family—were outside the jail and the county courthouse.

You have to understand downtown Los Angeles in 1969 and 1970. Around the courthouse was all concrete sidewalks and broad streets filled with traffic. It was dirty, as many cities are, with trash blowing into the gutters, and sidewalks stained with chewing gum and littered with cigarette butts. People did not linger outside. They quickly walked to their offices or meetings, not talking to each other, not looking up. The people walking into the courthouse were straightlaced, double-breasted types, Brooks Brothers shoes and shiny leather briefcases.

You can imagine how those attorneys and their staff reacted when Charlie's girls appeared each and every morning in flowing skirts, flowers in their hair, playing on flutes, dancing to music, both heard and unheard, and—finally—carving *X*'s into their foreheads in solidarity with Charlie Manson. It was quite a scene. For some, it confirmed that the hippies were taking over the world.

In early December 1969, one of Charlie's Family, Bruce Davis, surrendered himself in grand fashion on the street corner in front of the courthouse. Davis was wanted on a warrant for murder. Five television cameras were waiting for Davis and his bride, Brenda McCann, as Davis told the press he was giving himself up in order to "clear" Manson of the murder charges.

One reporter asked Davis why he surrendered and Davis replied: "They want to kill bodies, don't they? Isn't that what they're after?" He added: "Charlie would do it for me." His intent, apparently, was to testify and clear Charlie of any part in planning or executing the murders.

The strangeness of this, the theater of it, was like nothing I had seen before. The other reporters felt the same way. What we didn't know in the beginning was that this theater, this circus-like scene, would later be shrugged off as a typical day at the Manson trial.

If it was chaos outside the building, it was just as much of a madhouse inside. Hundreds of reporters and spectators were there, jostling for a space inside the courtroom, and sometimes fighting over that space. Reporters had flown in from all over the world, and many different languages could be heard daily. This was before cellphones, so the few payphones had long lines at any given moment. There was a press room in the courthouse, but the phones in there were also coveted—and guarded.

Everyone was scrambling for a glimpse of the man himself, Charlie, who was more than happy to add to the "street theater" the trial was turning into. He posed with arms out, as if he were being crucified. He routinely argued with the judge, dramatically throwing away a copy of the Constitution, once even jumping over the counsel table in an effort to stab the judge. His antics upset the courtroom more than once, which is likely why he kept having his privileges taking away.

Before I managed to get Charlie to talk to me, I was scrambling to get more information on the murders any way that I could. I remember clawing my way up a hillside in a skirt and heels, trying to peer into the Tate property without the police turning me away—which was tough, because the house was at the end of a cul-de-sac. I remember going through the Tates' garbage and pulling out film. I kept that film for decades. When I pulled it out to find out if someone could still see what was on the film, it fell apart in my hands. I had to throw it away.

I finally got a break, and found a neighbor who would talk to me. He said he heard screams from the Tate house at about two or two thirty in the morning, making the time of the murders no later than that. The police had the time of the murders earlier, but they had never talked to the neighbor. "If I had looked out the window," he told me, "I could have seen the murderers cutting the phone lines."

Why the police hadn't talked to him before I did made me question my long-time love of law enforcement. Another witness the police seemed to have "lost" was an eleven-year-old named Steven Weiss. He found the murder gun—a long-barreled .22 caliber revolver—behind his house about a month after the killings and immediately turned it over to the Los Angeles police. But the police didn't take him seriously, and when young Steven saw headlines about how the police were looking for the gun, he had to call and remind them that he had already turned it over. I certainly spoke with him—it seemed unreal that the detectives had not.

In yet another "miss" for the investigators, a television crew found a bundle of bloody clothes at the side of the road and turned it over to police five months after the murders. In trial, Linda Kasabian testified that she threw that bundle of clothes out the window of the car the night of the Tate murders, after she and the others had stopped and changed out of their bloody things. Had no one searched the roads to and from the Tate house? It was hard to believe.

In our first few meetings, Charlie was still acting as his own attorney. He had gotten his hands on the Grand Jury transcript. He said it was obvious that Sadie Atkins had been coached, that she appeared to be reading from notes.

"Sadie told those people what they wanted to hear. They coached her—and you can see it in the transcript. She says things like 'strike that' and when asked a question, says, 'Is that what you've got on your notes?' She's really been coached."

Charlie explained that he had spoken to a friend who had managed to get in to the jail to see Sadie. According to this friend, Sadie had been threatened. They had told her they were going to take away her baby, and she was frightened. According to Charlie, they told her they could get her a lot of money for her story—which happened. So she agreed to tell a story, and, right or wrong, Charlie was at the center of it.

In our second interview, Charlie opened up more. It was obvious he was testing his defense strategy on me. Sadie was lying . . . he was never at either of the murders . . . he was too small to do anyone any damage . . . anyone testifying against him was either coerced or threatened. Sadie, for example, was told that the authorities would take her baby away if she didn't testify against Charlie. Other girls—there were dozens living at the Ranch with Charlie—were interrogated for days until they agreed to testify against Charlie, and some of them were threatened with losing their children.

"They've taken one girl's baby at least three times. It really is a pretty sinister thing."

Coercing his girls was just part of it, according to Charlie. The prosecution, the judge, and law enforcement were all in on it, chasing away witnesses, threatening them, making it impossible for him to bring in witnesses to prove his innocence:

> They were just frightened to death, and most of them just ran away after that. There were a lot of people at the Ranch—sometimes there were close to 125 people that would come through there and spend a couple of days, then hike on. Kind of an open commune-like thing. It worked out pretty nice. But they scared the stuffing out of all those people and they're running all over the countryside.
>
> Now they have one witness of mine arrested on a phony charge, and they have an impossible bail on him and they're moving him from cell to cell. Another one they've taken to Independence [in central California, on the eastern side of the Sierra Nevada Mountains] and every time we send someone to Independence they move him to Lone Pine. They've got three witnesses locked up there. They're applying every bit of pressure they can.

In this second interview, Charlie told a story about attorney misconduct that was—at first—hard to believe. Months later, after I had seen how this case brought out the worst in almost everyone, I realized Charlie was likely telling me the truth. Charlie accused one of the lawyers who showed up in court of making up everything from being Charlie's attorney, to meeting with Charlie, to Charlie's level of education: "He says 'my client—I represent Mr. Manson.' He does not represent me. He went down and told the judge, 'Manson can't read or write, so he shouldn't be his own attorney.'"

I can tell you from personal experience that Charlie could not only read and write, he was also smart and savvy. He had an excellent vocabulary. He could talk about current events and history. He may not have had a lot of formal education, but he was sharp and intelligent.

He went on to tell another part of this lawyer's scam:

> He [the lawyer] brought a newspaperman in and said he was a friend of mine and wanted to make a deal with me. They said he could get $130,000 for my story and asked if I would give him my story. I told him "no, I don't want to give no one my story." He went out and wrote a prefabricated story anyway—a three-part story for a London newspaper and he made up all kinds of disaster-predictions, like everyone was afraid I was going to commit suicide, and all kinds of things he could think of that would be bad. . . . that people would want to hear.

Despite Charlie saying he didn't want to give his story to anyone, he was talking to me. And, it seemed, checking my reaction to see how his story was being received, trying out his testimony for trial. He tried making me feel sorry for him, as well: "Most people that go to jail—and society doesn't understand this—are generally people who have no one on the outside to help them—and I'm one."

Eventually, when he would say something like this, I would roll my eyes and say, "Gimme a break, Charlie," and he would give me a smile. But at this point, I was careful to give credence to his story. And so, he kept talking to me, and he double-checked on me by reading my paper as often as he could get his hands on it.

I used a lot of colorful language to describe the testimony at trial, including one that was plastered across the paper—and a number of affiliated papers across the country—in ninety-six-point type: "Wolf Pack Gang of Thrill Killers." Charlie mentioned it in one of his calls to my home. He said he had one of my papers. "You called us a wolf pack gang of thrill killers." There was a long pause. I didn't say anything.

"You wrote that?"

"Yep," I said, with a "what the hell" attitude I didn't feel. "Colorful isn't it?"

He laughed.

I liked Charlie, despite everything.

Our relationship was mutually beneficial. I landed headlines no other reporter could touch, and Charlie used the opportunity to tell his side of the story. Prosecuting attorney Vince Bugliosi hated it—and me as a result. He felt I was giving Charlie a chance to defend himself in print. The prosecution had created an elaborate theory of "Helter Skelter" to support his attempt at conviction, a theory Charlie openly scoffed at.

What did I learn about Charlie during those interviews?

Charlie was a very smart man, but with only an eighth-grade education. He had the handwriting of a ten year old, but the vocabulary of a college graduate. And perceptively, he was a genius. He had what I would call a high emotional intelligence. He could read a room or an individual with incredible precision. He watched you carefully, looking for reactions and hints as to how you felt, and he reacted accordingly. When he was focused, he was a force to be reckoned with.

But he wasn't always focused. Charlie could rant and ramble as if he were high or drunk, going on wild, long-winded tangents. He had outlandish theories about gender roles, minorities, sex, drugs, family, and the meaning of life. And he claimed he could talk with animals.

Charlie told me a story about a horse on the Spahn Ranch that was dying. He lay beside the animal stroking its head through the long night until it breathed its last. He told me about the wild burros in the desert whom he befriended and, he added, "They even would carry my baggage . . . whatever I picked up in the desert . . . and take it home for me."

Charlie was certain he could communicate with animals. He told me about going camping in the desert. He found a small watering hole and heard the coyotes yipping all around him. It was, he said, the only water in the area, so he moved about a half mile away and "called out to them in their own way." He told me:

> One by one coyotes quieted down. It took about a quarter of an hour, then everything was quiet. It must have been an hour later, I was sacked in for the night, when from down there by the water hole came one last howl from one of them that sure as hell said, "thanks, pal."
>
> I used to camp at that same spot often, always moving off from the water hole at night for the coyotes.

One day, Charlie said the coyotes reciprocated:

> One morning, when I awoke after having played tag with the park rangers the evening before, this big coyote came loping across the flats. I was standing in plain sight. He ran up to within about five feet of me and then stopped, staring dead at me, unafraid. This went on for about ten or fifteen seconds. He was angled towards me, and several times looked back the way he'd come, like he was trying to tell me something. All of a sudden it struck me that the rangers were coming, and as soon as that thought crossed my mind that big guy took off back in the direction he'd come from.
>
> I loaded my gear in the buggy and got out of there. About ten minutes later, I was stashed away nice and cozy on a slope hidden by some pines. Looking out across the desert floor, sure enough there came the rangers and from the very direction that coyote had come from to warn me.

This was the charming Charlie.

There was also the unpredictable Charlie, quick to anger—with me, with the judge during trial, with the girls when he still led his cult. But with me at least, the anger was more often like a summer squall, over almost as soon as it arrived.

His girls were not so lucky. Multiple witnesses said he abused them regularly.

According to some of the testimony, Charlie forced some of the girls to work on the Ranch while naked. No reason, just because he could. Another was told to work in the fields all day, then keep working all night as well. She did. His girls "gathered" things for him, stole for him, begged for him, and they all loved him.

He was a master manipulator. Not just with his girls, but also with his attorneys and his jailhouse guards.

So why did Charlie talk to me? I believe at first, he thought he could manipulate me. After all, I was a woman. But in time, I believe he grew to respect me and the job I was doing. Of course, neither of us forgot why we were there. He was getting to speak to the wider world, and I was getting to ask questions of the world's most infamous killer.

In early stories, I described him in colorful language: "the leader of a weird savage hippie cult," "hypnotic-eyed cultist," or "long-haired cult chieftain." Once, I added them together: "Shaggy haired, bearded Charles Milles Manson, the hypnotic-eyed leader of the nomadic cult . . ." As time went on and I got to know him better, the descriptions were more nuanced—in one story, I called him an "articulate hippie cult leader." But I knew how to write what people wanted to read. In one story, I started with a question: "Charles Manson—is he the world's hottest lover or the world's coldest killer?"

Some of the press criticized me openly, saying I was "too friendly" with Charlie and that was clouding my judgment. That was, to put it crudely, B.S., pure jealousy. Charlie never knew anything about me, he didn't know about my family, my background, nothing. At least not from me. Charlie called my home about three times a week, each time calling my newspaper's switchboard, and an operator would patch him through to my house. It was so frequent that my adolescent daughter would yell out, "Mom! It's Charlie again!" when she answered the phone.

I didn't "slip" and give him any ammunition, any personal information, because I never forgot that the man was in jail for multiple murders. When you're talking with people like that—even and especially Charlie and his girls—you keep them at arm's length.

But was Charlie a friend? I'd say we were friendly. We exchanged letters for years after his conviction and he remained an excellent source to me as a reporter—connecting me to other killers in jail, serving as a reference so they'd talk to me, and later discussing Lynette "Squeaky" Fromme's assassination attempt on President Gerald Ford.

Some have suggested I should feel guilty about giving Manson a voice during his trial. But I believe it is essential to find out what makes such men tick—how they think, how they operate and how they seduce others to kill. After the Manson trial, I did it with other accused serial killers. Bill Bonin, LA's notorious Freeway Killer, even gave me his handwritten confession, not only to the murders he was charged with, but several others.

I was good at my job.

But Charlie was different.

Charlie admitted to me that he had a "rotten past," but he also said he had "broken through," and he flashed me one of his best smiles. "My mother ran off when she was young and the rest of her family ended up in prison too. All of them ended up bad. But that goes way back. Her grandpa cut off somebody's head, and her daddy did something else. It was in the family."

Charlie's mother was Cathleen Maddox, who ran away from home with her older brother, Luther, just after she graduated from junior high in Ashland, Kentucky. It was while living a Bonnie-and-Clyde lifestyle—rolling and robbing drunks—that Charlie was conceived. Two years after his birth, a bastardy action was filed in Boyd County, Kentucky, and Charlie's father, listed as Colonel Scott, was ordered to pay twenty-five dollars, plus five dollars per month, for support of Charles Milles Manson. At the time judgment was granted, Cathleen Maddox had married William Manson, an older man who quickly disappeared.

When Charlie was only four years old, his mother and uncle were arrested for robbing a Charleston, West Virginia, service station and knocking the attendant in the head with bottles. They ended up in prison, and Charlie ended up with his maternal grandmother. He respected his grandmother. But—as he said—he had a "rotten past."

I don't think Charlie was at the Tate house on that August night in 1969. But he was a killer. He had a tough childhood and had been in and out of prison since the age of fifteen. A genius, a dreamer, a racist, a manipulator, a killer: Charlie was a complicated man.

2 A Little Bit about Me

When I entered the profession, women in a newsroom—if you could find any—were a rarity, a curiosity, and definitely not accepted by the men there.

Women were consigned to writing about cats or giant-sized squash or abandoned puppies being "mothered" by a prize pig. I refused to do that, but I did my share of obituaries and took my share of dictation from reporters covering fires or crimes of some kind. I got a little tired of that. Later—as my stock as a crime reporter began to rise—I made sure the person taking my dictation from the field was a man. It was a form of getting even.

I enrolled at the University of Southern California (USC) as soon as I could. All my life I wanted to be a newspaper reporter. There was nothing else. I dreamed of the scoops, the excitement. But the head of the journalism department didn't like women in journalism. I remember being a naive freshman in his beginning reporting class. He gave the class a set of facts: A family lived on Reef Inlet, a small island, close to the mainland and connected by a small pedestrian bridge. The mother was in need of some bread and milk from the store on the mainland, so she sent her seven-year-old daughter to get it. The weather was stormy, but it was a short trip. The girl apparently slipped on the wooden bridge and fell into the water and drowned. Write it, he said.

I did: a seven-year-old Reef Inlet girl, on an errand for her mother, drowned yesterday when she was swept off Potter's Bridge connecting her home to the mainland.

It had all the elements: who, what, why, where, when, and how.

When all the short paragraphs were turned in and he had a chance to look at them, the professor ordered me to stand. I didn't like the look in his eyes. Then he attacked, berating me for having no conscience. "You," he said, pointing at me, "blamed the mother for the girl's death. Do you know what you would put her through. . . ." and on he went. Finally, he said "sit," and I sat.

A couple of semesters later, I missed a French final, but I immediately spoke to the professor and he set a date for me to make up the exam. The only thing the chairman of the journalism department knew was that I got an incomplete in French class—and that was enough to try to get me thrown out of the USC School of Journalism. His first words to me were, "I finally got rid of you." By this time, I had learned to use my voice—unlike in that first class—and I said, "I forgot to take my final French exam, but I talked to Professor Belle, and he has set a date next week for me to make it up."

That was just in university. I could not imagine what I would be facing in the real world.

When I left USC, I couldn't get a job at a newspaper, so I took a job at KFI Radio. I began by writing public service announcements and graduated to writing two shows a day for their new FM station. It was fun, but I wanted the excitement of newspapers.

I talked my way into a job at the *Press-Telegram* in Long Beach. In the years that followed, the paper hit 200,000 circulation and was bought by Ridder Publications. It eventually became part of the Knight Ridder chain, the second largest chain in the country. So my stories, at least the good ones, were picked up across the country, and in some cases around the world.

Meanwhile, as a reporter, I was beginning to cover all types of stories. I spent some time as an editor on the suburban staff in charge of some twenty reporters. But I was still looked at as a second-class citizen—a woman. Even though I was in charge of twenty male reporters, editing their stories, assigning stories, and more, I was paid half—*half*—of what the reporters who worked for me were making. I was a bit resentful, but it really didn't worry me. I loved what I was doing and I knew where I was going.

But I think the editors felt I was getting a little too sure of myself. I needed a little humility. I think some of them felt I couldn't make it on the waterfront, the Los Angeles Long Beach harbor, one of the toughest—albeit best—assignments on the paper. They thought I might be able to handle San Pedro's

"Fisherman's Fiesta," but not the goon squads sent by the Chicago-Detroit strike breakers to break up the Longshoremen's Union.

But I knew I could. I grew up in San Pedro, in the harbor, spoke many of the languages, had relatives and friends who were longshoremen, fishermen, teachers, preachers, businessmen. It was my town. My harbor.

The press room was on the third floor of city hall annex, on the waterfront, one floor above the police station and four floors below the jail.

I walked into the room when I knew no one was there—I just wanted to see what I was getting into. I had run into most of the reporters who worked there, but I'd never seen the inside of that press room. At the time, there were ten newspapers in the area, covering the harbor. Many had two reporters working in the press room full-time.

The smell of stale cigarette smoke and stale booze—a room that hadn't been cleaned in years—hit me. But I expected that. I didn't expect it to be the pit it was, dismal, dirty, jammed with desks piled high with newspapers, torn telephone books, crumpled papers, half-filled coffee cups, and half-finished sandwiches.

Except for a narrow pathway between the door and the desks, the floor was no better.

The walls, ceiling, and floor were covered with pictures of women, most of them nude, pasted one on top of the other for lack of space. There wasn't an inch of bare wall. I felt better knowing they hadn't decorated the walls because I was coming. It was a product of years of rip and paste.

Only one piece of art was different. A framed sign reading "God Bless Our Happy Newsroom." The glass protecting it was broken. Later, I found out it was the result of a drunken brawl between two reporters. They both took a swing, missed, fell down, and knocked themselves out when they hit the floor. The picture fell to the floor along with them, skewering the frame and cracking the glass. But it was back on the wall.

The desk of the reporter I was replacing was in a corner, but I wasn't about to clean things off to find it. I figured that after five years as a newcomer, I would again have to pay my dues.

On Monday morning, when I walked back into the press room—my first day on the job—the whole rumple-suited harbor press corps and an assortment of police detectives were waiting for me, slouched in chairs, drinking coffee, talking on the phone, some arguing. I was expected. As I pushed open the door, the room quieted. I saw my corner desktop was clean, except for a lone, plastic geranium in a broken pot.

I could take that. Then I looked at the two walls that were "my corner." All the pictures of women were gone. Looking down from the ceiling and up at me from the floor and eyeball-to-eyeball from the walls were pictures of men . . . with very little, if any, clothes on. My face must have said what I was thinking. The laughter almost broke the windows. From that day on, I was on my own and had to make it without "special treatment" because I was a woman.

The first time I climbed a steep shipboard ladder, leading the pack to interview a renegade Turkish ship captain, was unforgettable.

The gangplank was almost straight up and I wasn't climbing fast enough in my heels and skirt. Grant MacDonald, an uninhibited *LA Times* reporter-photographer who had covered the South Pacific during World War II, was last in line.

Anxious to get on board, and thinking my heels and skirt were slowing me down, Grant looked up at me, screaming, "Neiswender, why the hell don't you wear pants?" His voice boomed across the harbor. To this day, I would give odds that the entire Turkish crew hanging over the side of the ship watching us spoke perfect English. I could tell that the howling longshoremen standing on the wharf understood the language.

No one gave me special treatment on the harbor beat, and it was the best beat a reporter could hope for. I have so many stories from those days, both comic and gory. What the editors didn't know—or didn't understand—was that the harbor was my home. If they wanted to scare me off, chase me back into motherhood and PTA meetings, they picked the wrong woman and the wrong beat. I wasn't cut out for the PTA, but I knew what I wanted, all I ever wanted: I wanted to be a newspaper reporter.

My professional peers on that waterfront were great reporters, and my cop friends, LAPD's Harbor Division, were the best. They taught me well.

And there was plenty to learn.

In the jammed harbor area there was crime and action—gang murders, Mafia murders, bank robberies, maritime disasters, collapsing buildings, drowning, longshoremen strikes, gang rapes, smugglers, and refinery fires. It was the best beat a reporter could hope for.

A few years later, I was ordered back to the main newsroom and was immediately sent off to cover postwar Germany. I sent back one story about ducking gunshots fired from across no-man's-land separating east from west. It was not the first time I felt lucky that my parents' ability to read English was limited.

I have interviewed everyone from criminals to presidents, including Josef Tito, then president of the former Yugoslavia. My first language was Croatian, so I tried that. But then I said I came from San Pedro, the city at the heart of the Los Angeles Harbor. He abruptly ended the interview and had two of his guards follow me for the rest of the day. He apparently thought I was a member of the Ustasha, the group that fought with the Nazis against him and his partisans. I didn't even get a chance to tell him that my uncle was his barber when he and his staff were headquartered on the island of Vis during World War II.

I picked grapes with Cesar Chavez, the hero of the farmworker union movement. I did a favor for Pat Nixon, who called to thank me and then sent an autographed photo of the president. My teenaged son threw it away during the Watergate scandal.

My credentials from Nixon's "Western White House" got me in to see the president of Costa Rica, who promised me a half hour of his time to discuss a scandal involving a local preacher with ties to southern California. We talked and laughed, and my tape ran out, so he reached into his desk and gave me a blank one of his own so we could keep talking. Great guy.

In 1971, Black activist Angela Davis was arrested because guns belonging to her were used in the armed takeover of a courtroom in Marin County, California. The prominent and controversial professor was held in jail for a year, and—just like Charlie—she didn't want to talk to any of the reporters trying to see her. But she called me and let me report on her situation. I had developed credibility in California's jails for being fair.

I went to Guatemala with my husband in 1976 to help him modernize the largest newspaper there. We were only supposed to stay for a few months, and in the middle of that time, a 7.5 magnitude earthquake shook the capital city. I was back on the front page of my paper again, reporting from a city that was half in rubble, tens of thousands dead. I went with two humanitarian doctors to bring food and water to the only place rescuers wouldn't go—to the city's isolated leper colony.

And my colleagues noticed. I won awards locally, then statewide, then nationwide, including the prestigious Sigma Delta Chi Award, the LA Criminal Courts Bar Association Journalism Award, multiple writing awards from the Associated Press and United Press International, and others. I received commendations from the California legislature and the key to the city of Los Angeles. I was the first woman named as president of the Los Angeles Press Club. I was a founding member of the prestigious Investigative Reporters and Editors organization.

Then there was Charlie.

Over the course of a very colorful career, Charlie stood out.

3 Charlie's Girls

I went to see Charlie in jail in February 1970, and he asked me, "You want to know what a real woman is?" I remember thinking it was a strange question, but when talking to Charlie, you took him on his terms. So I waited for the answer.

"A real woman is like this: she'll tell you she loves you and will do anything for you. Okay. Tell her if she really loves you to go out and get you another woman—one who's prettier than she is. If she really loves you, she'll do it—for the simple reason she wants to please you, and if that's what it takes—another woman, prettier, well okay. That's the kind of girls I had at the ranch."

Charlie told me he never told any of the Family to do anything: "I've always told people to do what they want to do—not what other people want them to do." I doubt that was true.

At the time of this interview, one of his girls—Sadie Atkins—had turned state's evidence (she promised to testify against the others in exchange for leniency in sentencing), even though she had said she loved Charlie Manson and would do anything for him. Her take on loving Charlie was obviously more than just finding him a prettier woman. She claimed Charlie told her to go out and kill, and kill she did.

Susan "Sadie" Atkins, known in the Family as Sexy Sadie and Sadie May Glutz, was fifteen when her mother died and her father left home in San Jose to look for work. Her criminal record began in 1966 when she was arrested for possession of a concealed firearm and receiving stolen property. When she got into trouble with the police, her father complained the courts were too lenient because they let her out of jail.

He may have been right. During the penalty phase, the officer who arrested Sadie in Oregon in 1966 for receiving stolen property and weapons charges says Sadie threatened to kill him. The officer testified that Sadie said she would have shot and killed him, if she had the opportunity. Sadie herself testified during the penalty phase, telling the jury that the Tate-LaBianca murders "ain't no big thing." Vince Bugliosi called her on that: "But seven murders, seven bodies—to you, that ain't no big thing?" "No," Sadie replied, "It wasn't at the time. It was just there to do."

She said she "didn't relate" to Sharon Tate "as being anything other than a store mannequin . . . She kept begging and pleading and begging and pleading until I got sick of it. So I stabbed her. . . . She sounded like an IBM machine—words came out of her mouth but it didn't make any sense to me." Prosecutor Bugliosi lost his temper with Sadie, shouting at her until the judge ordered him to calm down. It was one of many times that Bugliosi became entangled with the girls during their testimony, losing his temper, shouting, throwing things.

Testimony from one of Sadie's cellmates was nearly impossible to believe. The cellmate claimed Sadie was planning other murders, including Elizabeth Taylor, Richard Burton, Frank Sinatra, and singer Tom Jones. Sadie allegedly said she had "something unusual" planned for Jones, echoing the name of one of Jones's hit songs. I'm not sure how that testimony fared with the jurors, but I just rolled my eyes. The same witness testified that Sadie told her there was a huge hole in Death Valley where an entire civilization lived under the earth. The press corps often wondered why Bugliosi had called a certain witness. This was one of those days. But we wrote about it anyway.

Sadie was accused and convicted of the Tate and LaBianca killings, as well as Gary Hinman's murder, and her confession was instrumental in the arrests and convictions of other Family members. In 1971, on the stand during the penalty phase, she confessed to the Hinman murder and said she had been at the Tate house in 1969. Her testimony was cut short due to her uncontrolled sobbing, after she shouted at prosecutor Vince Bugliosi that the motive he claimed for the murders was "silly and dumb." At one point, Sadie testified that Charlie was the second coming of Christ. Later, she said she wasn't sure. Sadie died in prison in 2009.

But what of the others?

Leslie Van Houten was a legal secretary when she joined the Family and had been a high school homecoming princess. She came from a middle-class family, went to church every Sunday . . . and she stabbed Rosemary LaBianca fourteen times. She was convicted and sentenced to life in prison, but was released on parole in 2023.

Patricia Krenwinkel graduated from a Los Angeles-area high school and started teaching catechism. She flirted with becoming a nun, then attended a Jesuit college in the South. That didn't last, and she returned to Los Angeles. She testified that Manson was the first person who ever told her she was beautiful. She left everything behind—apartment, car, job—and went with Charlie to San Francisco, one of the first members of the Family. She was convicted and sentenced to death, as were the others, but all the death sentences were commuted. She has been in prison for more than fifty years.

Sandra Good came from a wealthy family and spent most of her life in boarding schools. She had some contact with her mother and stepfather, but not much. After she was arrested in a Death Valley raid connected with the Tate-LaBianca murders, her family posted her bail, then gave her $200 and told her that was the end of it. Sandy Good was eventually cleared of all criminal charges in relation to the Tate-LaBianca murders. She was the ringleader of the girls who spent more than nine months waiting on the street corner in front of the courthouse for news of Charlie's trial, at one point threatening to set fire to themselves if Charlie was convicted.

Linda Kasabian's parents were married only briefly, if ever. She grew up in New Hampshire and apparently saw her father only twice in fifteen years. She was married at sixteen, divorced shortly after. She had a child with her second husband, who brought her to California and then abandoned her. She found Charlie and the Family but seemed more interested in the easy availability of the drugs than the "family" part. After the Tate and LaBianca murders, she fled east, but was arrested, turned state's evidence, and became the main reason they were all convicted. Other Family members testified during the penalty phase that Kasabian was the "mastermind" for the Tate murders. All three of the girls said they had discussed the murder of musician Gary Hinman, and

Bobby Beausoleil's part in that murder, with Kasabian—and were told by Kasabian that she wanted to help Bobby Beausoleil get out of jail.

It was in March 1970 that the Family learned Linda Kasabian had turned state's evidence. Both the prosecution and Kasabian's lawyer denied it. Charlie denied Kasabian was ever really part of his Family.

"I didn't really know Linda too well," he told me. "I didn't know her well enough to tell her to go out and kill eight or ten people—or however many it was. Linda was just at the ranch about two weeks. Then she stole my car and left her baby."

He said she returned to the Spahn Ranch two months later to pick up her baby but never returned his car. As for testifying against him, Charlie figured Kasabian was under the same kind of pressure they leveled against Sadie Atkins.

"The girl has been under pressure from the district attorney's office for the past three weeks that I know of. In fact, her attorney has convinced her that he loves her and when the case is over he will buy a boat and they'll get her two children and sail off into the sunset."

How Charlie knew this is a bit of a mystery. He wasn't allowed to speak with Kasabian, even when he was his own attorney. But Charlie claimed that communications between him and Kasabian—as well as between him and other members of the Family—were continuing nonetheless.

In arguments to the jury at the end of trial, one of the defense attorneys argued that the girls were merely "mindless robots," trained to do whatever Charlie asked of them. I didn't see it that way. But another of the defense attorneys, Maxwell Keith, who was working for Leslie Van Houten jumped on the "mindless robots" defense, arguing to the jury: "If you believe the prosecution's theory, these female defendants are the extension of Mr. Manson—as if they were extensions of his arms and legs. If this is so, these female defendants cannot be convicted of premeditated murder or conspiracy to commit murder."

Keith came into the case very close to its end. He went on to argue that a woman couldn't have planned a crime like this:

> These are "thinking men's" crimes. You've got to think, plan, enter into talks about it and make up your minds. These people didn't have any

minds to make up, according to Mr. Bugliosi. I seriously doubt these girls had the mental capacity to harbor malice aforethought.

The minds of these girls—bearing in mind Mr. Bugliosi's arguments—were controlled by someone else. So not only did they not have the capacity to premeditate but they did not have the intent.

That is his argument—that is his baby—Mr. Bugliosi's. And if you're intrigued by his argument, you must acquit the female defendants.

Maxwell Keith described Linda Kasabian as "sinister," a thought shared by all the defense attorneys. Kasabian turned state's evidence early, with her lurid descriptions of Family life and the murders. She was young, cute, and dimpled in her first court appearance in December 1969, and she was heavily pregnant. Some of the allegations against the four defendants—Charlie and the three girls—were not corroborated by anyone other than Kasabian. While the truth of her testimony had been challenged due to Kasabian's drug use and sexual promiscuity, testimony showed that sex and drugs were part of the lives of all the defendants.

Linda Kasabian was the linchpin of the prosecution's case. During the trial I described her as a dimpled "buxom blonde," a relative newcomer at Manson's Spahn Ranch compound. She was given immunity for her testimony, and it was challenged by the defense attorneys as bought and paid for—she would say anything, the defense said, to keep her immunity deal in place.

Kasabian's testimony was full of inconsistencies. She testified that she was shocked and horrified at the Tate house, yet she went back again the next day to help kill the LaBiancas. She claimed Charlie tied up Leno LaBianca. Charlie was a small man, maybe 125 pounds. Leno LaBianca was six feet three inches tall and weighed about 200 pounds.

Kasabian testified that she loved Manson, and considered him "the Messiah, come again," and said Manson seemed to "generate love." But she also testified that she was an "emissary from God," on a mission to expose Manson as a false prophet and a devil. She claimed that she was afraid of the Family, but she had left her two-year-old daughter with them for months. She claimed she never used drugs at the Ranch, but others testified she was high all the time, including days in a row on LSD. And her ego seemed to gain speed through her eighteen days on the stand, as her wording became more colorful and the testimony appeared to be scripted.

As she testified about the night of the murders, Kasabian started to cry. But defense attorney Paul Fitzgerald didn't let this slide. He got her to admit that she had told this story multiple times and then asked her if she cried every time—or just in front of the jury.

Leslie Van Houten's attorney told the jury:

> There's something more sinister . . . Mrs. Kasabian is a sinister person, she always seems to land on her feet. With all these counts of murder and conspiracy she is free. She is home, wherever that is, doing whatever she wants to do . . . I suggest to you that if she attempted by her demeanor on the witness stand to leave the impression that she was a little girl lost in the woods and trying to find her way out, it was a facade. I find her wily, opportunistic, frightfully resilient. She bounces back no matter what she has done. I suggest she was driven by the strongest of human emotions—self preservation.

One member of the Family testified that Kasabian spent most of her time at Spahn Ranch high on LSD, taking the drug for days at a time, "lying around and watching the birds," ignoring her daughter. Kasabian herself said she had never taken drugs at the Ranch. Multiple witnesses challenged her testimony, but it didn't seem to damage her credibility.

Kasabian sobbed uncontrollably as she told the jury of the screams coming from the Tate home. She sobbed whenever she looked at photos or had to describe the killings. She cried as described how she looked into the eyes of one of the bloody and dying victims, Voytek Frykowski, as he stumbled out the front door of the Tate home, trying to escape from Tex Watson. Tex, she said, caught up to Frykowski and beat him in the head with the butt of a gun. Kasabian said she watched as Frykowski's girlfriend, Abigail Folger, also tried to escape, only to be caught by Patricia Krenwinkel. Krenwinkel ran up to Kasabian and asked her for a knife—Kasabian handed it to her. Abigail Folger was killed by multiple stab wounds. In all, there were one hundred and two stab wounds in the four victims.

But Kasabian herself escaped when the Tate victims could not. By the end of trial, she was living in New Hampshire with her two children. As Leslie Van Houten's attorney had said, Kasabian always seemed to "land on her feet."

She was vilified during the penalty phase. In one of the trial's many dramatic days, Kasabian was brought to the stand to testify for the prosecution. Irving Kanarek was cross-examining Kasabian, when Sadie Atkins apparently couldn't take anymore. Sadie interrupted the testimony by shouting, "You only got off by putting it off on Manson . . . admit it! Why don't you tell your part!"

Kasabian shot back, "I have! Why don't you tell your part?" Then she turned to Charlie, and shouted, "And why don't *you* tell your part?"

"Live with it," Charlie answered. "It's on your race."

Judge Older tried to restore order to the courtroom—it seemed he was always doing that—and Kasabian seemed flustered for the first time in the trial. And Kasabian had testified in the guilt phase of the trial for almost four weeks.

"This whole trip it's . . . whew. Really? This whole situation is insane," Kasabian said. Kanarek seized on that and asked what she meant by "insane."

"It's almost like it's unreal," she replied. "I know that it happened. I was never touched by anything like this before. It's hard to relate to after being away from it for awhile."

Manson interrupted again: "She means she never dumped her load on anybody else before."

So much for keeping order in the court.

Sadie Atkins was not as lucky as Kasabian. She cut a deal with the prosecution early on, in exchange for leniency. Prosecutor Vince Bugliosi would later refuse to honor that deal, insisting on the death penalty for the woman Charlie called "Sexy Sadie."

It was Sadie's testimony that led the police to Charlie and to the Spahn Ranch. While Charlie said Kasabian was only a hanger-on, not a "real" member of his Family, Sexy Sadie was a charter member. She was the snitch who led the police to the others, and it was her confession in Lawrence Schiller's book *The Killing of Sharon Tate* that ignited the fire around the Family that burned for the next year.

Sadie later recanted her testimony to regain the approval of the Family, but it was too late. The police took the clues she had given them and began building the case against the defendants. Charlie claimed Sadie had only confessed under duress when police threatened her child, but the confession was out there.

When the penalty phase of the trial began, Bugliosi had already said he was seeking the death penalty against Sadie Atkins. She took the stand so that she could tell the jury that she was tricked into confessing. In January 1971, Sadie was only twenty-two years old. By the time she died in 2009, she had spent forty years in prison.

The trial was hard on Sadie. In September 1970, about halfway through the trial, after complaining of stomach pains, she told the court she was sick and couldn't come to trial. She spent the day with her head resting on her arms, saying to the judge that she was "doing everything I can to hold onto my sanity."

Judge Older had her looked at by a doctor, who said Sadie was "articulate, lucid, and apparently perfectly healthy." The doctor said it was likely the pains Sadie complained of were psychosomatic.

Sadie would have none of it. Just before the morning session was done, she stood up, struggling, acting feeble, and threatened to scream if she wasn't removed from the courtroom, saying "I can't take it any longer. Your Honor, if you don't get me out of this courtroom, I'll start screaming."

I felt the same way. Sadie Atkins's "illness" was hard to believe. But again, it was good copy. If nothing else, the Manson girls could be counted on for some drama to keep the stories on the front page.

Later, Judge Older put Sadie on the stand to testify as to her physical condition. She started testifying from the wheelchair used to bring her into the courtroom, but the judge was obviously annoyed by her theater and ordered her to get up and get into the witness box. Sadie told the skeptical jurist that her pain came "from another dimension": "After I gave birth to my first child, I went into a state of delirium, I went into another dimension. The same thing is happening now—and I'm doing everything I can to bring myself out of this. It's not nice there. I'm doing everything I can to hold onto my sanity."

She said she hadn't eaten for days. The judge agreed to a three-day recess. When she returned to court, the histrionics were not over: she came into court sobbing, allowing herself to be helped to her seat by two deputies. Despite the gag order, prosecutor Aaron Stovitz called Sadie Atkins "better than [actress] Sarah Bernhardt." It was that offhand comment that got Stovitz kicked off the case, leaving Vince Bugliosi alone in the spotlight.

Later on, Sadie admitted to killing Sharon Tate as Tate pleaded for her life, crying that she wanted to live, to have her baby. Sadie admitted stabbing the woman over and over and that it meant nothing to her, that the life of the unborn child meant nothing. Yet Sadie claimed she was coerced into testifying in front of the Grand Jury because authorities threatened her with the loss of her own baby. And Charlie had called that coercion "sinister."

With all the crazy theatrics of this trial, sometimes we—the press—forgot about the victims. Sharon Tate, whose baby lived on for fifteen minutes after its mother had died in a frenzy of blood and screaming . . . heiress Abigail Folger, who tried to run . . . Jay Sebring, who was a famous "stylist to the stars," a karate expert, without an enemy in the world . . . Rosemary LaBianca and Leno LaBianca, who ran grocery stores and loved horse racing. We heard about these people, but they almost became background noise as we listened for nine months to stories of orgies, drug use, and the Spahn Ranch commune, and every day, we passed by Charlie's girls in front of the courthouse, *X*'s scratched into the flesh on their foreheads.

It wasn't only Sexy Sadie who led the police to Charlie. One of the defense attorneys, Paul Fitzgerald, had Patricia Krenwinkel examined by a doctor in December 1969, when Krenwinkel was in jail in Mobile, Alabama. I managed to get a copy of that report, and it shows that Krenwinkel told the doctor many details of the Tate killings, which had happened only a few months before. The doctor wrote:

> She says that she had just come off an acid trip and was feeling bad when she was awakened by Charles [Manson], that he told her to accompany Chuck [Charles "Tex" Watson] and do what was told. She, Chuck, Linda and Susan then went to a house and she says that Chuck killed the

> people there. She says that she did not do any of the murders. She says that Chuck shot several of the people, that Charles was not there. She says as soon as they arrived at the place that Chuck shot one man so she, Patricia, then realized that something bad was going on. They then went into the house and he killed the other people. He asked her to help him hold the ropes. She says that she and the other girls helped him and that he told one of them to write something on the door. They did not talk much about their actions afterward "Charles said not to."
>
> They left the house, went back to the desert "I was glad to get to the desert." After they returned to the desert she was upset she says and cried. Sometime later Charles told them, she says, to get in the car again with Chuck and do what he said and that again they went and killed two people. She said that she worried about the people "it'd be easier to have Charles kill me." . . . "Charles said nobody could touch us." She said she had never been to the Tate home before and knew none of the people.

Krenwinkel claimed that she fled Los Angeles because she was worried Charlie was going to kill her. During the doctor's interview, she claimed to be hearing Charlie speaking to her, and that Charlie was saying that she will never be able to get away from him, that there is no place to run or hide, that he has control of her mind and that he will kill her.

The doctor's conclusions were that Krenwinkel was mentally ill: ". . . she shows a schizophrenic reaction, mixed type, with emotional flatness and withdrawal, impaired judgment, loosening of thought processes and auditory hallucinations. I do not state with a certainly that this psychosis existed at the time of the alleged murders but it is obvious that at that time she was a severely emotionally disorganized personality and probably psychotic." An image of the doctor's report is included in this book. It's worth a read—Krenwinkel told the doctor all sorts of things she would later deny.

The judge completely disregarded the psychiatrist's conclusions when Krenwinkel tried to change her plea from not guilty to not guilty by reason of insanity in January 1971. The hearing on the change in plea took place behind closed doors, but Krenwinkel's attorney, Paul Fitzgerald, expressed in open court that Krenwinkel herself was not happy with the change, which might explain the quick denial.

During the penalty phase, and over the objections of her attorney, Krenwinkel told the jury that she quit her job as an insurance company file clerk and joined the Family to become a "nymph in the woods." She left her five-day-a-week job to "run through the woods with flowers in my hair . . . as Charlie played a pipe."

The jury had found that Krenwinkel was the only one of the girls to take part in both the Tate and LaBianca killings. Her story of love and joy was a little jarring, knowing what we did:

> I was living in a small apartment and working every day doing exactly what everyone else does, but I was very unhappy. It was nobody's fault because my parents tried to do their best for me. I didn't go out much. I stayed home a lot. But I had a friend, Bill, who lived a few houses down the street. One night, I went over and there were two girls there Mary [Brunner] and Squeaky [Fromme] and Charlie was sitting on the floor playing his guitar.
>
> I loved his voice and I loved his playing.

She paused, looking at Manson who was at the counsel table.

> Charlie came to stay at my apartment for four days because the girls took off for awhile. I saw somebody who stood on the truth. He stood behind everything he said. He let me sit and talk out anything I wanted to and he understood. He showed me how to love—I had been held in for so long. We laughed and had a good time.
>
> When Charlie's girls returned they said they were all leaving and I insisted on going along. I took a change of clothes and I left. I was doing what I wanted to do when I wanted to do it. We started traveling up and down the coast—mostly in the woods. We'd run like nymphs in the woods and I began to experience the creatures of the woods.

> Living in Los Angeles is like living in a big concrete madness. This was the first time I had started to feel free—to experience the sky and the sun and clean air.

This idyllic picture changed when Krenwinkel admitted to being at both the crime scenes. But she had no remorse.

In chilling unemotional tones, Krenwinkel detailed to the jury how she ran down and killed Abigail Folger on the front lawn of the Tate house. The next day, she went to the LaBianca home and stabbed Rosemary LaBianca to death. She then stabbed Leno LaBianca in the stomach with a barbeque fork, and used his blood to write "Rise," "Death to Pigs," and "Helter Skelter" on the walls.

"It was right," she said. Her quiet certainty was bizarre.

The prosecutor asked, "Are you willing to suffer the death penalty for what you did?" Krenwinkel's response was quick: "Yes."

She claimed she was in an LSD "fog" during both crimes. "I have taken so much acid," she said. "I am acid. I never come down."

She made this statement during a "protest" by Charlie from his seat at the counsel table. I called Charlie a "master puppeteer" when I wrote the story. It started when Charlie, who was sitting quietly, raised his left arm, finger extended. He kept it up for more than half an hour, until the judge called a recess. Judge Older ignored it, as he ignored much of what Charlie did in court.

But the girls didn't ignore it. First Sadie Atkins, then Leslie Van Houten, rested their elbows on the arms of their chairs and extended their forefingers. Then, from the witness stand, Krenwinkel half-raised her left arm, with her forefinger extended.

I had to wonder if this was a sign, or a ritual. Was Charlie revisiting some hypnotic trigger he had created at the Ranch? I never found out.

Leslie Van Houten was the youngest of Charlie's three girls on trial. She was only twenty-one years old when she testified during the penalty phase. While Patricia Krenwinkel described the murders in a cold and unemotional way, Van Houten was the opposite—she laughed, giggled, and waved her hands about while responding to her attorney's questions.

Van Houten had been named homecoming princess in her freshman and sophomore years of high school. She did well in school until she met a boy—an old story. She threw her arms over her head, laughing, saying he was something special, but "he won't have anything to do with me now."

The boy introduced her to marijuana and LSD when she was only fifteen years old. She liked it and decided to "take as much as I could."

"It was just like a pretty guy," she said, apparently trying to be helpful. "It's there. . . . someone asks, 'you want to try it?. . . . You say, Yeah! Sure! It wasn't an escape. It was complete curiosity."

Van Houten dropped out of school and hung out with the boy for a while, ending up as a secretary for a guru-based fellowship. Then she moved on, drifting to the Haight-Ashbury district of San Francisco where she met Bobby Beausoleil. Eventually, Van Houten met up with a group from the Spahn Ranch in a San Jose prune orchard where their bus had broken down.

"I hesitated, but I stayed with them. It was like I had known them forever," she said. She met Charlie at the Spahn Ranch, but at first she had little to do with him: "He was just one of the men there, but I felt very good feelings toward him—he gave a feeling of strength. We didn't speak for a long time but he wasn't any different from the others. Sometimes at night, he'd play music and we'd all sing, but I never paid much attention to him during the day."

Van Houten seemed to fall into killing the same way she had drifted into drugs: it just happened. She testified that she killed Rosemary LaBianca "because it just happened." During the penalty phase, she testified in line with the testimony of Sadie Atkins and Patricia Krenwinkel: Charlie never told them to kill anyone.

Charlie's girls were outside the courthouse as well.

One of the girls, a pregnant eighteen-year-old named Ruth Ann Morehouse, testified during the penalty phase. Like the others who had camped outside the courthouse for almost a year, Ruth Ann had a cross etched into her forehead. When she testified, she was nine months pregnant and expecting the baby at any moment.

The press corps wondered, crudely, when and where the child had been conceived.

Ruth Ann testified that she was living on the street corner in front of the courthouse, and had been since she found out Charlie was in jail. Her testimony was strange—she was there to tell the jury that "anything you do to any of us you do to us all." She certainly sounded like she had absorbed Charlie's "I am you and you are me" routine.

During the last days of the trial, while the jury was deliberating over whether to give Charlie the death penalty, the girls on the street corner threatened to burn themselves to death, should the jury come back with the gas chamber. The five women shaved their long hair, and said they would embroider a vest for Charlie with it. Sandy Good, the twenty-six-year-old daughter of a wealthy San Diego stockbroker, spoke for the group, saying the change in appearance was to shock people into realizing that an innocent man was on trial.

The spectacle did nothing. The jury came back with the death penalty for Charlie and his three girls, and they took very little time to do so. The girls on the street didn't set themselves on fire.

I just couldn't work up any respect for the girls. Charlie was smart and thoughtful, and although I could never get behind his "I am you and you are me" routine, he was an interesting man. The girls were just flaky. In the case of a couple of them—the killers—I felt nothing but disgust. And this is why.

The coroner's testimony is often ignored when talking about the Tate-LaBianca trial, but Los Angeles County coroner Dr. Thomas Noguchi was a compelling witness. A quiet man, he spoke softly with an accent that often made it difficult to understand some of the terms that he used. But his testimony was so empty of emotion, of the theatrics we had come to expect, that what he said carried a lot of weight.

Abigail Folger died of drowning. She drowned in her own blood, because she was stabbed in the face and neck over and over again, twenty-eight total stab wounds, with one of the stab wounds causing hemorrhaging into her windpipe. If that hadn't happened, she would have died from the stab wounds to her aorta or her stomach.

Polish playboy Voytek Frykowski was stabbed fifty-one times, shot twice, and beaten over the head. "Overkill," said Dr. Noguchi, who testified that Frykowski would have died from any number of the wounds he received.

Jay Sebring was also, as the doctor put it, the victim of "overkill." He had been severely beaten about the face, then shot several times. Any of three of the bullets in his chest would have killed him.

As for Sharon Tate, she was stabbed sixteen times, then—as she was dying—she was hanged. Sadie Atkins said Sharon begged and pleaded for the life of her child. Sixteen times she was stabbed, and then they hanged her as she was dying. It was inconceivable.

It was Sharon's blood the girls used to scrawl "pig" on the door.

Rosemary and Leno LaBianca fared no better. They were stabbed multiple times, and electric cords pulled tight around their necks. After being stabbed twenty-six times, Leno had the word "war" carved into his stomach with a carving fork from his own kitchen. We were told that Rosemary wasn't dead immediately after the stabbing, with the lamp cord tied around her neck. She crawled for a few feet before dying. They knew that because she had dragged the lamp behind her.

Later in my career, I was given a handwritten confession by Freeway Killer Bill Bonin, detailing dozens of torture deaths of young men and boys. I was in a Los Angeles County courtroom when I heard the screams of women killed by Lawrence Bittaker, who tape-recorded his torture-murders. Those were horrible, but the Tate-LaBianca deaths stand out, even now.

I haven't talked about Tex Watson, also part of the Tate murders, because he wasn't at the Manson trial. Watson was twenty-four years old at the time of trial, an honor student, an all-American, a Texas high school football star, 6 feet 2 inches tall, and—apparently—insane. Two psychiatrists examined Watson right after he was arrested and declared him unfit for trial. When Watson was arrested in Texas in December of 1969, he weighed 195 pounds. After ten months in jail, he weighed only 110 pounds, and the psychiatrists declared his life was in danger. His appearance was so shocking that when Watson first appeared in Judge Older's Los Angeles courtroom, Irving Kanarek objected, on grounds Watson's appearance, by itself, was prejudicial: "I will ask for a mistrial if Tex Watson is brought before the jury. It's a show. There's no probative value whatsoever. It's like a vaudeville show."

The jail physician first claimed Watson to be "competent, coherent and capable of standing trial." He also concluded that Watson was sane at the time the crimes were committed. But the physician's report also shows that the doctor based his conclusions almost exclusively on the transcript of Linda Kasabian's testimony. A week later, that same jail physician reported that Watson was listless, flaccid, and refusing to accept any food, even spoon feeding. The doctor's about-face was startling: "It is imperative that the defendant gets psychiatric and physical care as a life saving measure." Watson was immediately transferred to Atascadero State Hospital in central California until he was fit to try.

Tex Watson had everything going for him before he hooked up with the Family. He was a scion of a pioneer ranching family, handsome, wealthy, respected. When he was first arrested, his dad said, "I don't think he did it. I've raised a good bunch of boys. My sons have never been in any trouble." There couldn't have been more differences between Charlie's youth and the childhood of Tex Watson. But Tex admitted to doing Charlie's bidding or—as he said at the time—the devil's work.

Trial testimony showed that Tex Watson was one of the Family members present at both the Tate and LaBianca murder homes. He was described as aggressive, crazy, and very violent. He was the wheel man the first night, driving the girls to the Tate house. In the driveway of the El Cielo house, he came across young Steven Parent, who had been visiting the caretaker. Watson shot Parent and then helped the others kill Sharon Tate and her friends. He did the same the next night, driving the killers to the LaBianca home, and helping the girls with the murders there.

A year after the Manson trial, Tex Watson was tried on his own. He was adjudged fit to stand trial and convicted of the seven murders, same as Charlie and the girls. The Watson trial was a much less theatrical affair—no one leaping over the counsel table to stab the judge, no crosses carved into foreheads, no pretending to be crucified. Just a trial.

Tex Watson was sentenced to death, but like the others, that was commuted to life in prison. In 1975, he became a "born again" Christian and an ordained minister in 1983. He married, and he and his wife operated a prison-based ministry. He fathered four children while in prison, three boys and a girl. He is, at the time I write this, alive and in prison, having been denied parole eighteen times. He even sent me Christmas cards now and then.

Charlie always stressed that he never ordered anyone to kill, but during the trial, he told me that he had "ordered" the girls at the Ranch to talk to me. So I drove up to Spahn Ranch to interview any Family members who weren't in jail.

Lynette "Squeaky" Fromme—later convicted of taking a shot at then-President Gerald Ford—showed us around. My photographer and I walked into the Family's "Gypsy Hut," a small trailer set off by itself from the main house. Tacked up on the door was a poster that looked like a wanted poster and read:

> Reward for information leading to the apprehension of Jesus Christ. Wanted for sedition, anarchy, vagrancy, conspiracy to overthrow the established government.
>
> Dresses poorly said to be carpenter by trade. Ill-nourished. Has visionary ideas. Associates with common working people, the unemployed, bums, aliens. Believed to be a Jew. Alias Prince of Peace, Son of Man, Light of the World.
>
> Professional agitator. Red beard. Marks on hand and feet the result of injuries inflicted by an angry mod lead by respectable citizens and legal authorities.

Squeaky said the Family thought the description fit Charlie. During the trial, one of the cult members, Brooks Poston, said he had an "epiphany" that Charlie was Christ, when he saw a man kneeling at Charlie's feet, and heard Charlie promising the man eternal life. Manson himself told the Family that he had experienced "dying on the cross" during a psilocybin trip. All I could do was shake my head.

The girls had made cookies for us, but I told the photographer not to eat a thing. I had heard about spiked food, including a warning about an LSD-spiked hamburger. The four girls there that day all had a lot to say about Charlie, the

Ranch, and their friends in jail. I was furiously taking notes when—in the middle of the interview—I was told there was a call for me at the main house. I was told Charlie wanted to speak to me.

My photographer was puzzled. "How'd he know you were here?"

"You tell me," I answered. "And how did he get to a phone? They won't let him make calls out of the jail anymore."

Charlie just wanted to know if everything was going okay, if the girls were cooperating.

"How the hell did you know I was here, and how did you get to phone?"

He didn't answer.

So after telling him the girls were being very helpful, I went back to the "Gypsy Hut," where I was told by all four of Charlie's girls that he never told them to do anything. "A long time ago," one of them explained, "Charlie said he needed a shirt. So I went and made a shirt for him. He didn't tell me to make a shirt."

All four of the girls were nodding, and all agreed: Charlie never told them to do anything. Not to get him a shirt. Not to kill anyone.

The girls—I don't think I ever got their real names—started peppering me with their love and reverence for Charlie.

"A lot of people think Charlie took kids from fine homes, put them in a terrible place and did awful things to them. Or that we lie around in bed all day and get loaded . . . It's not true," said one.

Another said, "All of us were just wandering around, alone, not having anybody and not thinking there was any love left in the world, when all of a sudden, there was this little man sitting there just playing his guitar and saying 'It's okay' and loving us. He loves us so much, you just can't help but love him back." Their tone was one of reverence. To his girls, Charlie was more than a lover, more than a brother or a father. He was more like God.

Katherine "Gypsy" Share was one of the girls there that day. Later, she would be accused of being part of a complicated plot to break Charlie out of prison. That day at the Ranch, she was just another of Charlie's girls, anxious to make me understand what a treasure he was: "I was born in France . . . I was one of the first people to come over without any parents. I was a war baby. I don't look it, but I'm twenty-seven, as I was in that war thing." Gypsy claimed she "just sort of drifted" to Charlie: "We've all been—all our lives—coming together from all over the world. Just getting together. They [the Family] started calling me Gypsy about three years ago. I guess it's because I play the violin—like a gypsy does."

A few years later, I interviewed prosecutor Steve Kay, who said Gypsy was a "dangerous girl," and that she had a plan to hijack a plane at Los Angeles International Airport. She was going to kill a passenger every hour until they released Charlie. He told me the hijacking scheme was Gypsy's plan, and she was the ringleader. Kay thought Gypsy was at the very least an accomplice in the murder of Shorty Shea, a ranch hand at Spahn Ranch, but they couldn't prove it. That day at Spahn Ranch, Gypsy was as sweet as a person could be. Polite and accommodating. She was, like many of the other girls, a good actress. But some of the things she said about Charlie and life at the Ranch were very hard to swallow.

Almost a year later, Gypsy Share was called into testify during the penalty phase of the trial. Threatened with the loss of her baby, who had been born while she was in jail on unrelated charges, Gypsy sobbed through her testimony. She said Linda Kasabian was the mastermind of the Tate-LaBianca killings. She testified that Sadie Atkins and Leslie Van Houten were the killers, and they had been in a "planning session" with Kasabian a few days before the killings. Manson, she said, had nothing to do with it. Gypsy said Kasabian had told her that she was "involved" with the Hinman killing and that she needed to get Bobby Beausoleil out of trouble. Gypsy Share testified—and most of her testimony was through tears—that Kasabian asked Gypsy to kill for her:

> Linda asked me to go out and do some killings. It's hardly describable. Everything had gotten out of hand. The only thing on my mind was to go away, so I told her I didn't want to have anything to do with it. I didn't want to know about it. I just wanted to go away. I just walked off and kept on walking. I went into the hills and sat on a rock and tried to understand. I really didn't have anywhere to go, and I loved everybody

> at the Ranch. I stayed there (in the mountains) a long time—a couple of weeks—and when I came back, she was gone.

Charlie had told me that the authorities were threatening the Family members with loss of custody of their children. It certainly was the case for Gypsy and her baby Phoenix.

Brenda McCann didn't get a colorful nickname, but she had multiple other names, as her arrest records showed:

> When I was sixteen, I was kicked out of the house and I didn't have anywhere to go. What had been happening was that my parents had been saying to me for months, "If you don't like it here, just get out." So finally one day I did just that—I took off and was walking around saying to myself, "hmm, where to now?"
>
> Then I met Charlie. He was sitting in the back of a big school bus playing a guitar. All he said was "Come on in and listen." I did. He played the guitar for a while, then Squeaky came in and we just all fell in love with each other. So I stayed. And I've been here ever since.
>
> We're just young people and we realize that falling in love is a beautiful thing, and it's a good thing. There's no reason why we just can't fall in love with each other and just stay together. People do it all the time. They fall in love and feel just because they fell in love with someone else that they have to drop the person and go through all those bad feelings and everything. But they do it—they drop the second person and go on to another. In the meantime, they're losing all those beautiful relationships they had.
>
> We don't do that. So what we are really is a family. They labeled us that. We never called ourselves that. But actually we're more of a family than any people I've ever seen. We're each other's brothers and sisters. We're everything to each other.
>
> This is the only family we really have, and the only family that love each other enough to sit down and talk to each other about problems. If we

need a father, then one of the guys is a father to us. If we need a brother to romp around with us—we've got a brother. If they need a sister just to sit down with, the boys have a sister. But it's also love. Love has gotten into it, and it's also a lover, also a wife and a baby and taking care of them.

It's everything."

When I went to the Ranch that day, only a handful of Family members remained. After the arrests, and the absence of Charlie, many of the Family chose to leave. At one point, there were many children at the Ranch, but that day there was only one: Elf. He had a given name—Chosen—but Brenda said they called him Elf because they said he looked like one:

> We look at him as a little person rather than a baby. We don't treat him as a baby, we let him do what he does. . . . So many people say he needs a father, but if they can only see when four or five boys—men—who love Elf, playing with him all the time. They could see that he has more fathers than anyone could ever hope for, and ones that really love him and will stay with him, who don't go out on drunks, and don't beat him and who don't leave, but stay with him, and are there whenever he needs a father.

There had been quite a few babies at the Ranch, with colorful names like Pooh Bear, Sunstone Hawk, ZeeZo, and Phoenix. One of the girls testified that Sunstone Hawk was Mary Brunner's baby and emphasized that they didn't know who the father was. In testimony at trial, one member of the Family said Brunner's baby was "Pooh Bear" and was in charge of everything at the Ranch. I later found out that Mary Brunner's baby was Charlie's son. The girls called the babies the "love babies" and said they were in charge of everything. They said they followed where the babies told them to go.

The girls then started telling me about "free love," and how sex and love intersected at the Ranch. Charlie was at the center of that intersection. "He loves us so much," they told me, "you just can't help but love him back." This didn't ring true, because I knew that Charlie would tell his girls to have sex with men who came to the Ranch, in exchange for getting work done. But this is what I was told:

> A lot of people talk about free love and they have no understanding of it, absolutely none, because in their mind they equate it with sex. Actually what it is, is real love, because each of us are in love with each of us. And it's not a casual thing. We don't let anybody in to make love to anybody. They've got to love us as much as we love each other.
>
> A lot of times, men would come around and they'd see a bunch of girls. They'd come in and say, "I want one of these girls—ya know, free love." They'd be on downers or drunk or something.
>
> Charlie knew we could take care of ourselves, but sometimes he'd help us and go out in front for us—because no one else would. He'd go out in front because he saw it needed to be done. He'd say, "Wait a minute here. This is no whore house. Either you love these girls as much as I do or you leave. And loving these girls as much as I do is giving up your whole life for them. It's being everything to them—being their whole family, brother, father, husband, everything."

I heard this, knowing that other Spahn Ranch residents had already talked about Charlie giving the girls to men who came to the Ranch in exchange for things he needed. Some of those residents said that Charlie routinely abused the girls. This didn't match.

Gypsy told me, "The Press has gotten nothing—nothing but people's imaginary stories—anything that sounds wild and horrible. They have no idea what's going on. No idea."

What was going on, both Gypsy and Brenda told me, was that Ranch life was continuing, without some of the Family members, even without Charlie.

"We are all each other. I may know how to handle this, someone else may know how to handle that. Someone is a good organizer, someone is a good cook. We all exchange what we have and give it to the center. We work for ourselves—and whoever is with us is ourselves."

Obviously Gypsy had learned Charlie's "I am you and you are me" speech well.

"We're not a commune—that's what people don't understand. It's not just some place where someone can flop and do their own thing. When you come here you give of yourself. People are not used to being given heaven. You give them heaven and they don't think they're worth it, so they tear it apart. You have to really love yourself. Get to the point where you can be together with yourself and love yourself in order to love anyone else."

They said Ranch living was heaven, everyone loving everyone else:

> We'd get up when the sun comes up, and the girls would cook, go out and get food, sew and play. We had lots of time to play because there were a lot of girls here then, and there was always someone who wanted to cook and someone who didn't feel like it.
>
> As soon as it got dark, we'd all sit down and eat. The girls would have been cooking for two or three hours, making a big banquet. We had a party every night. We'd all sit around in a big circle. When there were a lot of people we'd sit around in the saloon. We'd sit in a big circle and pass all the food around and we'd eat and relax after a hard day's work.
>
> Then Charlie would pick up his guitar and I'd pick up a violin and somebody else would pick up a flute and someone would pick up another guitar and we'd all start singing. We'd sing about anything that came into our minds. A lot of times we'd just sing what was in the air. . . . things like "I can't remember when my mother told me to shut up and get out of here. . . . I can't remember when she said I was no good." It was like a therapy thing—what was in our minds, about our past, our parents, what was happening her, about climbing the mountains, about anything that was in our mind.

Charlie usually led the singing, as he led life at the Ranch. Brenda and Gypsy told me Charlie was there to make sure everything went well, for George Spahn, for the girls, for the horses. Everything.

> Charlie would get on a horse now and then and work with the cowboys. He'd spread himself thin over everything and make sure everything was

running smooth. He didn't try to change anything, he just saw how it was going and saw that it was running smoothly.

Charlie is always concerned . . . not in a worried way. But he's concerned if everyone's happy and everything's ok. He's never told anybody what to do. He asks questions: "How's this? How's this going?" and "Are you happy?" and "Is this going ok?"

As the girls spoke, I couldn't help but remember the bodies of Leno and Rosemary LaBianca. Leno was the son of Italian immigrants and ran a grocery business. He was involved in raising thoroughbred horses, a dream of his. Rosemary and a partner ran a clothing store. The two lived in Leno's childhood home, a house he purchased from his mother, the house he grew up in. He bought that house in 1968. A few months later, Charlie sent his Ranch girls and others to the LaBianca home. The LaBiancas were slaughtered. The idyllic Ranch life Gypsy described had no connection to the girls sitting in the LA County Jail. Or to Charlie.

Obviously, the tripe that Gypsy was trying to feed me was aimed at making Charlie seem like a saint. Instead of feeling better about Charlie, I left the Ranch a little bitter. I had been set up. And I walked away wondering how in hell Charlie had managed to call me while I was there.

It made a good story, though.

4 The Family

In early 1970, Charlie explained to me how the Family got started:

> The last time I got out of prison, I had a real ego collapse. I finally realized that I wasn't big and strong and handsome. I finally realized I was just me. So I went up the road kicking a can and whistling. I had found me. I had no illusions about myself.
>
> I saw a boy sitting by the side of the road. He had no one. No one wanted him and he had nowhere to go. He asked if he could join me. I said, "No, join yourself, but if you want, we can walk together." So we did. Then we found another one—a girl who had nowhere to go. A nobody. Somebody nobody wanted. And she walked with us.

That, claimed Charlie, was the beginning of his Family.

The three made it to Haight-Ashbury and to what Charlie described as "those beautiful people": "There was no rejection. There was just plain acceptance of me, as I was, for what I was. Instead of smallness and rejection, I found love. No one cared if my hair was longer than theirs, or that I didn't dress like they did. There was no stigma because of differences. We all loved each other."

At the Spahn Ranch and later at the Barker Ranch in Inyo County, Charlie said things were the same—everyone loved everyone else—and the people felt as he did. More and more "nobodies" came to stay with the Family. And while he claimed he only "cleaned the toilets," there was never a question as to who was in charge. Ruby Pearl, who helped manage the Spahn Ranch, said Charlie was the leader of the Family. She said Charlie "had a real good disposition, never aggressive or bossy." She said that anything Charlie asked Family members to do, they did: "They never refused. If any of them didn't do it right away, they were condemned by the others. Like if they spent money and Charlie needed money, that was terrible. They were supposed to give it to Charlie right away. Everything they had they gave to Charlie and he decided what to do with it."

According to Ruby Pearl, the girls got money from their parents. She cashed the checks, so she knew the amounts, sometimes as much as $1,000. The checks never bounced, she told me.

Ruby Pearl had a front row seat to the Family's activities: "They had no religion that I know of. They sang and played guitars but no chanting or that stuff. There were ten or twelve or fifteen of them—not many. There was never any trouble here." So it would seem the Charlie may have been telling the truth. At least in the beginning, he created a Family that lived in harmony.

During the penalty phase of the trial, Lynette "Squeaky" Fromme testified about what a good person Charlie was. Squeaky was there from the beginning and told the jury how she went with Charlie to Haight-Ashbury, where they picked up Mary Brunner. The three of them spent some time in Mendocino, then drove to Sacramento where they exchanged their car for a "big, black school bus." They took the bus to Haight-Ashbury. Squeaky said, "There were a lot of kids around there just trying to get away from that life. We took anyone that wanted to come."

Squeaky and Charlie met Patricia Krenwinkel in Los Angeles, and Squeaky described her as just another girl, looking for the truth, peace, and love. As for Charlie being the leader of the group, Squeaky barked out a quick "no," saying, "We were just riding the winds. Charlie is a man and we were all looking for a man who would bathe our feet in his love, but wouldn't let us step on him."

But people didn't want to read about Charlie's "good side." They were much more interested in his dark side. My editors loved the dark stuff, and asked for more, yet when I wrote the gory details from the trial, they would edit it, to clean it up, to make it more family friendly. This was in 1970, after all, and we were decades away from the uncensored explosion of "true crime" on the internet. While the public was anxious for all the details of the murders, the orgies at the Ranch, the drug use, and Charlie's stranglehold on his Family members, the stories I wrote were toned down to make them more palatable for the public . . . and, I'm sure, toned down for the advertisers.

In December 1969, before Charlie and his girls had been charged in the Tate-LaBianca killings, the press had managed to get to some of the Spahn Ranch cowboys to talk. And they had a lot to say.

Juan Flynn claimed Charlie had tried to kill him. He called Charlie a "Svengali" who could get anything he wanted from anyone in the Family: "He once put several of his girls in a hillside cave with only water, for a week. They stayed." He made it clear that "nobody disobeyed Charlie": "I can't say anything good about that guy. He tried to kill me twice and tried to take over the Ranch and everyone in it. We still don't know what happened to one of the ranch hands—I've told the police about that."

Flynn was referring to Shorty Shea, who was murdered: "Charlie said once he was 'striking knives into Shorty' but I thought he was only trying to scare me. Shorty didn't like the hippies around and he said so. If he had decided to leave the Ranch—even though he wouldn't say goodbye to anybody—he would have taken his guns. They were his whole life."

The cowboy was at Spahn Ranch as Charlie's hold over the Family members grew:

"He got a lot of girls first, then began to bring in the men. He called the men Zombies. I guess because they couldn't do what they wanted to do. Charlie would get them around a fire at night and chant . . . they'd all chant . . . then they'd all go to bed. There was a lot of gang sex stuff. He tried to get me to join. He said the only rule was that there were no rules."

Flynn said he joined the commune for a while but ended up in the hospital. He said that put an end to his participation: "I think that's part of it. These people get these diseases and they don't believe in doctors. It gets to the stage that it affects their minds. They had sores all over their bodies."

Flynn claimed Charlie had studied Scientology and was a "top man" in that cult. Flynn said Charlie used Scientology techniques to manipulate the Family. Charlie never told me anything like that. And where would Charlie have gotten the money for Scientology? That was the problem with so much of the trial testimony—what was true and what was just made up, to get attention or take revenge?

"Charlie believed in girls having babies," Flynn said. "One was born in a trailer on the Ranch. But he didn't believe in educating children—he only wanted them to serve him, like the girls."

Flynn said Charlie had once to put a knife to his throat, but he thought he was kidding, he didn't think Charlie "had the guts" to do it. Another time, Charlie came into the barn with a pitchfork: "I'm a little bigger than he is so he changed his mind and put the pitchfork through a rooster that was just sitting there."

Flynn said he and Charlie were always at odds, and that when Charlie got mad at Flynn, he would take it out on the girls, slamming their heads against the road or against a car door.

According to Flynn, when Manson called himself Jesus Christ, Flynn believed it: "His favorite quote from the Bible was Revelation 9: 'Neither they repent of their murders, nor their sorceries, not of their fornication, nor of their thefts.'"

Several years after his conviction, I spoke with Charlie again. He hadn't changed much. Rambling, talking about the past and present at the same time, he was still as enigmatic as he ever was. I found a transcript of that meeting. It is not dated, but it is clearly post-conviction. Charlie's own words explain the world he created for himself, before the murders.

This material was never printed in my newspaper because Charlie wasn't "news" anymore, and also because of what he chose to talk to me about. He first wanted to talk about the start of the Family, which came together in his San Francisco days:

> The Family was a name given to a group of people who lived together in a school bus. Owner's papers were in the glove box. There were no rules except the rules of the police, when the Family was stopped time after time.

No one who lived in the bus called the group anything—it wasn't organized. It was made up of people who accepted themselves. Once in a while someone who didn't like or accept themselves would ask, "Can I come?" . . . no one was refused. Once a man insisted on coming because it was snowing, he said he was cold. So one of the Family got out with his guitar and let the man get on. He then went to a place and played his music and people gave him food. He got a ride to LA, and beat the bus there by three days. . . . he had a good time while waiting for the bus. Sometimes people would hitchhike to where bus was going to be, and sometimes the Family went for days without talking much, just traveling from place to place. . . . like living in group therapy all the time. The people who didn't like or accept themselves generally went away with some dislike, or excuses why we weren't his brothers or sisters.

There were times when the number of people well outgrew the bus and we would split up . . . give the bus away . . . and then like magic it would find its way back and a group would form. The bus was even stolen twice. No one reported the thefts because no one really cared where they were as long as they were happy. The bus always seemed to be there when it was time to move. The last we heard of it, a group called the Eternal Family in Oregon had it.

Charlie's "I am you and you are me" routine never changed:

A family is made up of people who accept and love themselves to a point where they stand strong with their inner selves. One might say, "alone but alone together." A family doesn't need to say "good morning" every morning. Every morning is good, for all is good. We're brothers in blood and love, like in the bus. Out of the bus one is one, and when you're one, you're in the Family.

Many experiences went on in and around the bus. When the first sign of trouble came, someone would put on the bus driver's hat and say, "Let's go." We were always looking for a place where the man would just leave us alone. Three years, and we found no place to go where we could get away from the confusion. We met many buses, trucks, campers, hitchhikers, walkers, bike riders, and even once in Texas a small group of wagons, all looking for the same place. But we must face what we must face to be free from other people's concepts of freedom or what they think you should do.

At this point in the conversation, Charlie switched gears to focus on society's influence on the Family:

Once, we as the people made a man to watch over us and to protect us and it worked for a while. Now, he does not watch over us anymore, he just watches us every moment. . . . every move we make, and says we must do as he says. He has all the funds of the army pointed at the people. The only thing the people know is what they are told. If they knew what they're not told they would get buses too and try to get away from the madness.

We could save you a lot of trouble. We can not hide and soon you will be deeper in the trance. They look at me and say I hypnotized people. . . . I can't even spell it. But one thing I learned in twenty-one years in one prison or another, the people are the ones who are hypnotized. Not only are they unaware of what is happening, but they're more in jail than the people who think that they are in jail.

Brother, there is a big lock on most of the minds you see. The smarter you may think the person is, in schools and in books, the less he will tell you that you can believe or know. Because, with all he has learned, he has only that one never knows. He'll say to you, "To love is really to know." When you love and you know love, there is nothing more. Love is all, all is love, the circle is complete, another falling star. When you see you, then you'll see us, and then we are all a big family. Those who see and those who don't. . . . no leaders and no followers, just people together wherever they're at in space makes no difference. We are still one in love.

To us, we have always and will always be together as one, and since they need to give us a name, it seems they have picked the "Family."

This last part of his talk was typical Charlie, his "you are me and I am you" speech. I had little patience for this, but I learned to let Charlie be Charlie. Sometimes in the middle of his proselytizing, I would often get something I could use in a news story.

As far as I could tell from reading everything the other reporters had on the case, and from my own investigations, the Family was just Charlie and whoever was with him at the time. Even so, the police, sheriff's departments, and other reporters insisted on linking the "Family" with crimes all over the West.

5 Gary Hinman, Shorty Shea, the Symbionese Liberation Army, and More

Charlie told me that the police and sheriffs were trying to pin every random murder in the country on him—and he wasn't wrong:

> Some atrocious murders were perpetrated. So they say, "Well, we've got to find somebody, so we'll take these people here"—meaning us. But the murders are still going on.
>
> You know the machine will not admit that it's wrong . . . will not say, "We have got the wrong people . . . the killers are still on the loose." They're covering up the thing as much as they can.
>
> I read a small article in the paper where some people were killed in San Francisco, and "pig" was written on the wall. We've never heard any more about it. It was a very small article in the paper and it only ran one day. Then some friends of mine told me some people were killed in Santa Barbara—after I got in jail—and they're still trying to blame it on me.
>
> Then some people back east were stabbed and "pig" written on the wall. Then there's this guy named Scott . . . this guy's supposed father was related to an uncle that was named Scott, so maybe I had something to do with that.

It was true—it seemed the Family was being investigated every time a murder was committed. But there were other killings attributed to Charlie and his followers, murders that have largely been forgotten.

After the Tate-LaBianca trial, Charlie was tried and convicted of the murder of Gary Hinman. LA County prosecutors claimed he was responsible for killing the musician just weeks before Sharon Tate and the others were murdered. They argued that Charlie ordered Hinman's murder, just as he ordered the Tate-LaBianca killings.

The allegations came out in the murder trial of Bobby Beausoleil, one of Charlie's Family. The prosecution claimed that Charlie personally mutilated Hinman with a sword, then ordered him put to death. According to witnesses, Charlie had gone to Hinman's home in Topanga Canyon—then a bohemian enclave in the Santa Monica Mountains—and without warning, slashed Hinman in the face, cutting off his ear and cutting into the muscles of his jaw.

The critical testimony at trial came from Mary Brunner, a Family member for more than a year, and the mother of Charlie's child. She testified that Hinman was held prisoner by Charlie, Beausoleil, and Sadie Atkins. But she said she never saw Charlie with the sword.

Much later, in March 1971, Brunner recanted all of her testimony, saying she wasn't at the Hinman home, and she couldn't place Charlie at the house either. She testified that police officers had warned her before she gave testimony in connection with the Hinman murder that "I would be arrested if I didn't incriminate Manson."

The prosecution presented evidence that Beausoleil got a phone call: Charlie said to kill Hinman. And Beausoleil did, later confessing to the crime. He stabbed Hinman twice in the chest, and then walked outside to let the others know. But the sounds of Hinman's last gasping breaths were unpleasant to hear, so Beausoleil went back in and held a pillow over Hinman's face. Beausoleil was not the brightest of Charlie's followers, and he was still carrying the knife used to kill Hinman a few days after the murder. Police stopped him while he was driving Hinman's car. Beausoleil was arrested and charged with murder.

Beausoleil was convicted and sentenced to death. More than a year later, in 1971, Sadie Atkins told the court that she had killed Hinman. That didn't fit with the Beausoleil and Brunner testimony, but that's what Sadie said. She had a habit of confessing and later recanting. But she said Charlie told her to scribble "witchy" sayings on the wall of the Hinman house, in blood, and she did.

During the penalty phase of the trial, several people—including Sadie Atkins—testified that the motive for the Tate and LaBianca killings was to try to get the police to release Bobby Beausoleil. Apparently, the thinking was that if other killings also included "witchy" sayings on the walls in blood, then the police would think that Beausoleil—who was in jail for the Hinman murder—was the wrong guy. To me, this motive sounded far more plausible than the "Helter Skelter" race war theory that the prosecution dreamed up.

Charlie claimed that Sadie Atkins had been coerced into giving testimony against him in the Tate-LaBianca murders, pressured by being told that she would never see her children again. In the Hinman case, Mary Brunner's mother testified that her daughter had also been coerced, in the same fashion as Sadie Atkins—by being told that her child, Manson's child, would be taken away from her forever.

The theory was that Charlie wanted Beausoleil out of jail. At the same time, Charlie wanted to send a message to a record producer named Terry Melcher. Charlie had met Melcher in the house that would later become the home of Sharon Tate and Roman Polanski. Charlie was angry at not getting a record contract from Melcher, and he left a "warning" at Melcher's new home in Malibu. It didn't work, so he sent his followers to Melcher's old house to kill those inside. Charlie decided this would send a strong message to Melcher, and get him the record deal he so desperately wanted.

Melcher got the message. He left town.

I think a big part of the motive behind the Tate killings was an effort to cast doubt on Beausoleil's involvement with the Hinman killing. The "witchy" sayings on the walls of the Hinman house were also now on the walls of the Tate home. The writings were intended to link the Hinman and Tate murders and convince the police that Bobby Beausoleil was not guilty.

Unfortunately, Sadie Atkins hadn't left enough "witchy" messages on the wall of the Tate home. This was apparently the reason for the murders of Leno and Rosemary LaBianca. According to Sadie, Charlie wanted more "witchy" statements in blood, to confirm the link between the Hinman murder and the Tate-LaBianca killings. It was at the LaBianca home that "Helter Skelter" was first associated with Charlie and his "Wolf Pack Gang of Thrill Killers." They wrote it in blood, on the refrigerator, all to connect the Hinman murder with the Tate-LaBianca killings, in theory to get Bobby Beausoleil off the hook.

After the Tate-LaBianca trial was concluded, Charlie was also brought up on charges that he murdered Shorty Shea. According to members of the Family, Sadie Atkins lured Shea to a remote spot on the Ranch. There, at the request of Charlie, he was murdered, only two weeks after the killings at the Tate house.

Charlie told me in March 1970, in one of my first jailhouse interviews with him, that a "motorcycle guy" killed the cowboy and sometime stunt man:

> Here's how that happened. There was a motorcycle guy that got into an argument with this man. Him [Shea] and this man went off and they were fighting. I don't know the outcome. When this thing [Charlie's arrest] finally came out, the motorcycle guy stepped forward and said, "Well, I think Charlie did something to that man" and they took his word, so they went looking for the man.
>
> Here's my thinking: maybe the guy that told police did something to the man. It's very possible that he could have hit the guy on the head or something or got into a fight with him and shot him, then went and buried him and stepped forward and said, "Oh, yeah, I know Charlie's killed this guy," trying to cover up his own tracks. But I really don't know.

At his parole hearing, Bruce Davis said Charlie told him, Tex Watson, and Steve "Clem" Grogan to kill Shea. According to Davis, Charlie Manson handed him a machete, but he didn't use it. But Charlie was present, and according to Sadie Atkins, Charlie bragged of cutting Shea into pieces. In 1977, eight years after the murder, Shea's remains were found next to Santa Susana Road, just outside the boundaries of the Spahn Ranch. Clem Grogan had drawn the sheriff a map. Shea's injuries corroborated the reports from Davis, Sadie, and Clem Grogan: Shea had been stabbed multiple times, with chopping wounds to the chest and blunt force trauma to the head.

In 2008, a crew of forensic experts went to Charlie's camp in Death Valley and found evidence of more murders. Armed with the latest in forensic technology, a cadaver-sniffing dog, and an anthropologist, they searched the area of Charlie's last campsite, the Barker Ranch in Death Valley. With them was Debra Tate, Sharon Tate's little sister. Almost forty years after the Tate-LaBianca killings, headlines once again shouted Charlie's name. One read: "Experts Find Possible Evidence of More Manson Family Murders."

An AWOL Marine named Vernon Plumlee joined the Family before the Tate-LaBianca murders and was brought in to testify about Shea's murder. On the stand, he said that a number of other Family members disappeared or were killed. Christopher Zero left the Ranch and was found dead from a gunshot wound in Venice, California. Family members said he was playing Russian roulette, but Plumlee said he knew Zero well, and Zero would never have done that. He testified that a "real pretty girl" called Yellowstone drove off in a truck with a Family member and never came back. No one ever explained where she had gone. Despite this—as with so many other Family members—Plumlee respected and admired Charlie.

This was one of the difficulties in dealing with Charlie Manson. In person, he was charming, rakish, intelligent. But the evidence was strong that he was also a killer: violent, unpredictable, and cruel.

A side effect of the Tate, LaBianca, and Hinman killings was that law enforcement started to see Charlie's handiwork everywhere.

In 1969, there was a killing in Kentucky, and the local papers found more than a dozen witnesses who swore they saw Charlie Manson in the area in the spring of 1969, when the man was murdered. The victim died by multiple stab wounds, and there were enough links to the Tate murders that the Los Angeles Police Department began to look into it. In an interview with Kentucky's *Daily Independent*, prosecutor Aaron Stovitz said that both Manson and the victim were apostles of the Universal Life Church.

In 1972, a couple was murdered in Stockton, California, and three women were arrested who had *X*'s carved into their foreheads, the same type of *X* that Charlie's girls had carved into their foreheads during trial—two of the women arrested had direct links to the Family. Two men arrested had the symbol for the Aryan Brotherhood—a white racist organization—tattooed on them. The motive could have been racist, or it could have been a thrill killing. It didn't matter. The headlines screamed out the link to the Manson Family.

In the fall of 1979, a sheriff in Humboldt County was up in arms about a forty-acre property in his territory that he called "a sort of spa for radicals," naming the Symbionese Liberation Army or SLA, the Tribal Thumb (a revolutionary group in the San Francisco area), and the Charles Manson Family as some of those who used the "spa." Seattle police then linked the groups to a jailbreak in King County, in which one prisoner was killed and seven others were wounded.

Charlie's Family wasn't a "leftist group," as the Humboldt sheriff thought. It was just a group of men and women dedicated to Charlie. They took orders from Charlie, they stole for Charlie, they had Charlie's children. A greater political movement was not part of the "free love" community at the Spahn Ranch. Charlie was starting to talk about his predications of a coming race war when he was arrested for the Tate-LaBianca murders, but the Family was only a family because of Charlie's control. In my opinion, none of the theories attributing other crimes to the Family after Charlie was put in jail in 1969 were correct. I don't think it was organized, like the SLA for example.

Eventually, a woman was arrested for the Kings County jailbreak and killings, and the police linked her to Charlie through a woman who had been associated with the Family—Gypsy Share. Gypsy and the woman had worked together on a credit card scam, but the Gypsy connection was the only link to Charlie's Family.

The headline on my October 1979 story concerning the SLA and the Manson Family was simple: "SLA Joins Manson: Now What?" I wrote that both local and federal law enforcement officials were saying that the SLA and the Family were banding together in an effort to free Charlie from prison. The basis for this was tips from "street sources," hinting that the Family had recruited new members and had connected with the SLA. They cited the Gypsy Share credit card scam as evidence of a crime spree that included bank robberies. Unnamed informants claimed the money raised was being funneled into a "Free Charlie" fund, which would also be used to free certain SLA members.

The plan never came to anything, but whether because of law enforcement or because the informants were not telling the truth, we'll never know.

Even so, every time someone was arrested who could be tied to Charlie Manson, the Family, or Spahn Ranch, the police seemed to think that it was a coordinated effort by Manson Family members, or that Charlie was masterminding the crimes from prison. Charlie was certainly capable of it, but I don't think he did. By the time he started serving time after the trial, he was on a different path.

That didn't stop others from copying the witchy and bloody scrawling on the walls of the Tate, LaBianca, and Hinman houses to further their own plots. The worst was Jeffrey MacDonald.

The Jeffrey MacDonald matter was one of the most disturbing cases I have ever covered. He killed his pregnant wife, hitting her with a two-by-four that fractured her skull and tore the skin off to the bone. Then he broke both her arms as she tried to fend off more blows. Not satisfied, he stabbed her over and over in the neck and chest. To make sure, he stuck an ice pick into her chest twenty-one times.

He then did the same to his five-year-old daughter. The child's skull and face were shattered. Her cheekbone could be seen poking through her skin. He stabbed her repeatedly in the neck, cutting her windpipe and arteries.

He left his five-year-old's room and walked into the room of his two-year-old daughter. He picked her up and put her across his lap, face up, and stabbed her repeatedly. The autopsy showed defense wounds on her hands—she had tried to stop her father from killing her. He turned her over and stabbed her in the back, over and over. Then, in a bizarre twist, he put the girl's body back in her bed, covered her up, and put her bottle next to her.

Jeffrey MacDonald was a doctor working for the Army Special Forces. After he finished the murders, he went into the bathroom and punctured his lung, and he added a few superficial wounds to make it look as if he had been in a fight. As his final touch, he returned to his own bedroom and scrawled "Pig" in his wife's blood on the headboard of their bed. This happened on the East Coast, in North Carolina.

MacDonald told the police that Manson-type hippies had attacked his family, and the police started down that road, chasing—again—after Charlie and his Family. So I asked Charlie about it.

"All the murderers I know," he said casually, "would go after the husband first. He'd be the biggest one in the house. He would have been killed first. Not left alive. I'd take a long look at him if I were the cops."

I interviewed MacDonald when he moved back to the Long Beach area from North Carolina. He had started a new life, but there was still a lot of interest in him as a suspect in the killings. During the almost two hours that we talked, MacDonald was absolutely cold in his description of the murders of his family. He never referred to them by their names, or as his "wife" or his "daughter." He only referenced the tragedy as "the homicides." He was as cold as Sadie Atkins describing how she stabbed the pregnant Sharon Tate. There were far too many similarities for my comfort. The MacDonald murders and others are detailed in my book *Assassins . . . Serial Killers . . . Corrupt Cops: Chasing the News in a Skirt and High Heels.*

Ultimately, Charlie was right. It took almost ten years, but MacDonald was finally charged and convicted with first-degree murder of his wife and two daughters. "Blame it on the Manson Family" could only go so far.

Fig. 1. Mary Neiswender at the *Press-Telegram* shortly after she began (ca. 1951). Neiswender had editors hovering over her for the next thirty-five years. Authors' collection.

Fig. 2. Staff of the *Independent Press-Telegram* in 1952. Mary Neiswender is seated at the back, the only woman for several years to come. Authors' collection.

COLUMBIA UNIVERSITY IN THE CITY OF NEW YORK

PULITZER PRIZE NOMINATION

WE WISH TO ACKNOWLEDGE YOUR NOMINATION OF

Mary Neiswender

FOR A PULITZER PRIZE IN JOURNALISM

We appreciate the interest which prompted you to bring an example of distinguished journalistic achievement to the attention of the University.

Awards are made by the Trustees of Columbia University on the recommendation of the Advisory Board and are announced on the first Monday in May. All exhibits become the property of the University.

Secretary, Advisory Board on the Pulitzer Prizes

We received the following material on February 1, 1971:

☒ Nomination form ☒ Biography ☒ Photo ☒ Exhibit

☒ Your entry is complete.

☐ Your entry is incomplete. Please submit missing material.

COLUMBIA UNIVERSITY IN THE CITY OF NEW YORK

PULITZER PRIZE NOMINATION

WE WISH TO ACKNOWLEDGE YOUR NOMINATION OF

MARY A. NEISWENDER

FOR A PULITZER PRIZE IN JOURNALISM

We appreciate the interest which prompted you to bring an example of distinguished journalistic achievement to the attention of the University.

Awards are made by the Trustees of Columbia University on the recommendation of the Advisory Board and are announced on the first Monday in May. All exhibits become the property of the University.

Secretary, Advisory Board on the Pulitzer Prizes

We received the following material on January 30, 1974:

☐ Nomination form ☐ Biography ☒ Photo ☒ Exhibit

☒ Your entry is complete.

☐ Your entry is incomplete. Please submit missing material.

Fig. 3. Mailed postcards announcing Mary Neiswender's two Pulitzer Prize nominations. Authors' collection.

WALTER CRONKITE SELECTED FOR JOSEPH QUINN MEMORIAL AWARD

XXXI — No. 1 JANUARY, 1981

Walter Cronkite has been selected as the third winner of the Joseph Quinn Memorial Award to be presented at the Greater Los Angeles Press Club's annual awards banquet Feb. 28 at the Hyatt Regency Hotel.

"We are delighted that Walter has agreed to personally accept the awards," President Bill Farr said in announcing Cronkite's selection for the award established in honor of the late Joe Quinn, deputy mayor and founder of City News Service.

Previous winners have been Dave and Cathy Mitchell, publishers of the Point Reyes Light who won the Pulitzer Prize for their reporting on Synanon, and Jim Murray, the much-honored spot sports columnist for the Los Angeles Times.

Presentation of the Quinn Award for Outstanding Contribution to Journalism will highlight an evening of awards for the best 1980 efforts of print and broadcast journalism.

Serving on the awards committee planning the February event are Lloyd Ritter, Frank Haven, Art Watkins, Jack Shepard, Jim Hurley, Irv Cuevas, Bill Ferree, George Bridges, Maury Green, Milt Transchel, Lew Hatfield and John McSweeney.

WALTER CRONKITE

FIRST WOMAN TO HOLD POST

MARY NEISWENDER ELECTED PRESIDENT OF PRESS CLUB

By SANDI GIBBONS
City Editor, Daily News

A few years ago, the late President Tito of Yugoslavia was visiting Los Angeles and the Independent Press-Telegram in Long Beach sent Mary Neiswender, its top investigative reporter, to cover the story.

Mary's parents came from Yugoslavia and she is fluent in the language. Those of us who have worked with her over the years figured before the day was over, Mary would be sitting on Tito's lap and doing an exclusive interview with him in Yugoslavian.

Well, it almost happened that way. As Mary tells the story, she asked Tito a question in Yugoslavian and spent the rest of the day being tailed by Secret Service agents who suspected she might be a spy.

Mary, assistant city editor of the IPT and new owner of KGUY, the

(Continued on Page 9)

MARY NEISWENDER
President

BOB VOIGT
Vice President

Fig. 4. Newsletter announcing the election of Mary Neiswender as president of the Los Angeles Press Club in 1981, sharing cover space alongside Walter Cronkite. Authors' collection.

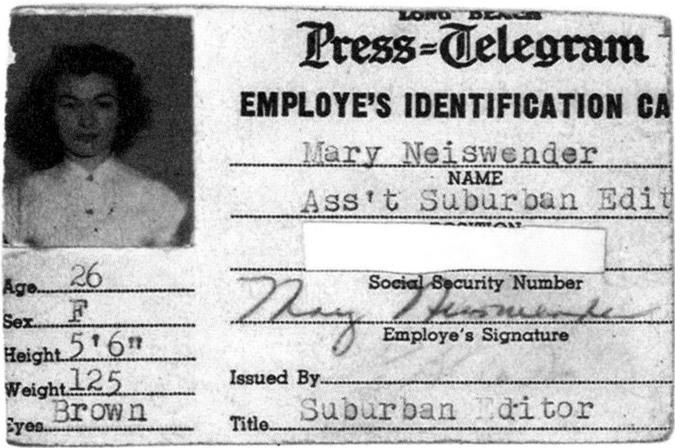

Fig. 5. Mary Neiswender's early press credentials. The one issued in 1974 was helpful in getting her to speak with the Costa Rican president at the time. Authors' collection.

TRAVIS — MAYBE THIS WILL SHOW I DID MORE THAN SEND A couple of Serial Killers to Death Row AND GOT CLOSE to PEOPLE LIKE MANSO.

JANUARY, 1982 THE EIGHT BALL PAGE SEVEN

The Year in Review!

came from Mary herself and other Press Club members.

She sent personalized letters to the heads of all newspapers, radio and television stations, wire services and some communications centers. Hopefully the work that was started on "Leave Your Mark" will continue in the future.

Then there was the Mexican Fiesta and the International Christmas Party—both adding significant funds to the building renovation. The list is endless.

But the club needed more than just reconstructive surgery to change its image to one of more professionalism. Emphasis was also placed on putting the tools together to encourage more working journalists, authors and the best in communications professionals to join the Press Club.

For the first time in the club's history an attractive membership brochure was produced as well as a professional-looking membership application. These will prove to be invaluable in increasing the membership over the next few years. Again—the emphasis was on the future good of the Press Club.

Mary Neiswender also insisted that the *8-Ball Monthly* be redesigned and its editorial content improved. I know—it seemed that she was always looking over my shoulder. She wanted more attractive paper at the same or less expensive cost, a new typestyle, the masthead redesigned, a more modern look overall—and emphasis on articles of interest to working professionals and those about important Press Club activities.

She was not satisfied until the *8-Ball* met her minimal requirements—even if it meant a total re-write of articles submitted to meet professional standards.

The new "image-building" didn't stop there. She appointed outstanding professionals to head a new Public Relations Committee—and they hit the trenches.

All Round Tables were preceded with press advisories and club activities and members' accomplishments were touted by news releases.

The point was to give the Press Club more visibility—and to promote it as an active, thriving center for working journalists, authors and others committed to excellence in communications and news dissemination.

And we can't forget the promotion of club reciprocity with press clubs all over the world—the success of the Headliner Banquet—and the reorganization of this year's (1982) Journalism Awards Contest to meet the needs of the

media in this area (something long overdue).

The fact is—Mary Neiswender's work in the past year is only overshadowed by her impressive career in journalism. To list all her awards and honors would be tedious—but here's a highlight of her highly respected career.

- One of the first women investigative reporters in the United States
- Nominated twice for the Pulitzer Prize
- Lauded by *Newsweek* for her coverage of the Charles Manson murders and called "The greatest reporter at the trial," by the *Los Angeles Free Press*
- Instrumental in legislative reforms which stemmed from several of her stories over the years
- Cited for her accomplishments in the California State Assembly and the U.S. Congress
- Winner of numerous awards from the Associated Press, the Greater Los Angeles Press Club, Pacific Coast Press Club, California and National Association of Press Women
- Named Outstanding Journalist in the State in 1972
- Given the L.A. Criminal Courts Bar Association's Journalism Award in 1975—the only woman and only person outside of metropolitan L.A. so honored
- Received the prestigious Sigma Delta Chi Award in 1980 ~~for "significant achievement~~ for "significant achievement and/or consistent performance as a professional journalist presenting the news with insight, perspective, accuracy and fairness"
- Named one of the most powerful women in the media by the *L.A. Herald-Examiner*
- Former Vice President ~~of and current member~~ of the Board of Directors of the Investigative Reporters & Editors (IRE)
- Recently given an award by the NAACP for her investigative work on the Ron Settles case

The list goes on and on! But Mary Neiswender is not merely a list of awards and achievements or simply a journalist with an impressive career. She is also a person who loves her family, is proud of her children, cares about her friends and respects and admires her colleagues.

She is unique among those we consider rare—those we admire for their vigor, their determination and their principles.

Therefore, on behalf of the members of the Greater Los Angeles Press Club, I would like to thank Mary Neiswender for what she has and continues to represent as a quality-oriented, professional journalist and for all the long hours of hard work she devoted to moving us "a few steps closer toward our vision for better things."

Fig. 6. The Los Angeles Press Club's newsletter featured Mary Neiswender's accomplishments upon her leaving the presidency. Authors' collection.

CONFIDENTIAL MEMORANDUM

TO: EVELLE J. YOUNGER
District Attorney

FROM: AARON H. STOVITZ
Head, Trials Division

SUBJECT: SUSAN ATKINS

DATE: DECEMBER 4, 1969

A meeting was held today in Mr. Younger's office, commencing at 10:20 a.m. and concluding at 11:00 a.m. Present at the meeting were: Mr. Younger, Paul Caruso, Richard Caballero, Aaron Stovitz, and Vincent Bugliosi.

Discussion was had as to whether or not immunity should be given to Susan Atkins in exchange for her testimony at the grand jury hearing and subsequent trial. It was decided that she would not be given immunity.

Mr. Caballero made it known that at this moment his client may not testify at the trial due to her fear of the physical presence of Charles Manson and the other participants in the Sharon Tate murders.

Discussion was held concerning the value of Susan Atkins' testimony. It was acknowledged by Mr. Stovitz and Mr. Bugliosi that the Los Angeles Police Department is grateful for her cooperation in the solving of the Tate murders and the LaBianca murders. Agreement was reached upon the following points:

1. That Susan Atkins' information has been vital to law enforcement in solving of this case.

2. In view of her past cooperation and in the event that she testifies truthfully at the Grand Jury, the prosecution will not seek the death penalty against her in any of the three cases that are now known to the police; namely, the Hinman murder, the Sharon Tate murders, and the LaBianca murders.

3. The extent to which the District Attorney's Office will assist Defense Counsel in an attempt to seek less than a first degree murder, life sentence, will depend upon the extent to which Susan Atkins continues to cooperate.

4. That in the event that Susan Atkins does not testify at the trial or that the prosecution does not use her as a witness at the trial, the prosecution will not use her testimony, given at the Grand Jury, against her.

an

Fig. 7. Memo from the confidential district attorney meeting at which it was decided not to seek the death penalty against Susan "Sadie" Atkins. Prosecutor Vincent Bugliosi refused to honor it, and Atkins was sentenced to death, along with the others, in 1971. Authors' collection.

Public Affairs Division · 150 North Los Angeles Street · Room 731 · Phone 624-5211 · Extension 3281

FOR IMMEDIATE RELEASE

August 20, 1969

FOR FURTHER INFORMATION CONTACT

Inspector Harold Yarnell
Administrative Inspector
624-5211, Ext. 3202

SHARON TATE MURDER CASE

This is an extremely complicated case involving five victims and no known witnesses.

We have only the physical evidence at the scene and the leads furnished by interviews with relatives, friends, neighbors, acquaintances, and those persons who have come forward.

Two lieutenants and seventeen sergeants have been assigned to the investigation and they have the entire staff resources of the Department available to them.

During the course of the investigation, more than two hundred persons have been interviewed and many remain to be interviewed.

We have the names of many individuals we would want to interview and some of them are in different jurisdictions. We have made inquiries of the authorities in those jurisdictions requesting assistance in locating those persons.

Mr. Harrigan was one of the individuals whom we believed could be of assistance to us. When Mr. Harrigan heard that our Department wanted to interview him, he came in voluntarily and was cooperative with the interviewing officers.

At this time we have no warrants of arrest for anyone.

Several rumors and speculation have appeared in the media and we feel compelled to comment on them in the interest of accuracy:

None of the bodies had wounds involving the sex organs.

Narcotics were found on the premises.

The word "PIG" written in blood was found on the premises. The letters were " P-I-G " not " P-I-C. "

At present, there is no evidence to connect these murders with any others.

We have no further details of the investigation to release at this time.

Fig. 8. The Los Angeles Police Department was not having any luck finding the killers in the early days of the investigation. This press release was issued August 20, 1969, about ten days after the Tate murders. The investigators' frustration comes through. Authors' collection.

FIRST HOMICIDE INVESTIGATION PROGRESS REPORT

DR 69-586 381

DECEASED:	LA BIANCA, Leno A. (CC #69-8859) LA BIANCA, Rosemary (CC #69-8860)
DATE AND TIME OCCURRED:	August 10, 1969, 0200/2230 hours
LOCATION OF OCCURRENCE:	3301 Waverly Drive
DIVISION OF OCCURRENCE:	Hollywood Division R/D 635

TO: Lt. P. B. LePage, Supervisor of Investigations, Robbery-Homicide Divn.

Sir:

RESUME OF THE CRIME

On August 10, 1969, during the early morning hours, the victims, Rosemary LaBianca and Leno A. LaBianca, were stabbed to death at their residence located at 3301 Waverly Drive by suspect or suspects unknown. The weapons used were a kitchen steak knife and carving fork belonging to the victims. Both victims were repeatedly stabbed and were found with pillowcases over their heads. Leno LaBianca's hands were tied behind his back with leather thongs. There was no evidence of forced entry and no indication of a struggle. The residence was not ransacked, but Mrs. LaBianca's purse had the appearance of being rifled and the wallet and contents are missing.

INVESTIGATORS AT THE SCENE

On August 11, 1969, 0015 hours, Sergeant D. Galindo, 3434, Robbery-Homicide Division, was notified of the double homicide occurring at 3301 Waverly Drive. Sergeant Galindo and Officer T. Taketa, 11091, Detective Headquarters Division, immediately responded to the scene, arriving at 0100 hours. Officer R. E. Miller, 11651, Detective Headquarters Division, subsequently arrived to assist in the investigation.

The crime scene was the residence of the victims, Leno and Rosemary LaBianca. It is a one-story, single-family dwelling located in a quiet high-income residential neighborhood. Directly west of the scene is the old estate of Earl C. Anthony; on the east and across the street are residences similar to the LaBianca's. On the north and directly to the rear is a sloping hillside with no immediate structures. The victims met their demise as the result of multiple stab wounds. Mr. LaBianca's body was located on the living room floor lying face up diagonally by the south couch. His hands were tied behind his back with leather thongs and his head was covered with a pillowcase. It appeared that he had been throttled with a lamp cord which was still attached to a massive lamp located beside the couch. A throw pillow from the couch was over his face. Mr. LaBianca had bled profusely

Fig. 9a and 9b. Pages from the homicide investigation for the LaBiancas. At this early stage, the police were convinced that the LaBianca murders were a copycat killing and unrelated to the murder of Sharon Tate and her friends. Authors' collection.

from the many stab wounds onto the seat cushions of the couch and floor immediately to the body. He was attired in pajamas with the button-up shirt partially open, exposing his rather large stomach.

There were four stab wounds in the abdomen. Inscribed by slashes on the exposed stomach area were the letters "WAR". Sticking out of the stomach, near the navel, was a bi-tined carving fork which had been pushed through the abdominal flesh to the bifurcation of the tines. On the coffee table, directly by the couch, was a freshly-printed version of the Sunday morning Los Angeles Times (8-10-69). In particular, the Sports section appeared to have been read. Mr. LaBianca's eye glasses were also located on the coffee table, indicating that he was sitting on the couch reading the Sports section. There was no indication of a struggle in the living room or dining room portion of the residence, and nothing appeared to be disturbed except for a tapestry that had been removed from the north wall in the living room and placed resting perpendicular against the same wall. Where the tapestry had hung and above several paintings were the words, "DEATH TO PIGS," printed in blood. On the south wall of the living room directly to the left of the front door, the word "RISE" was printed in blood. On the kitchen refrigerator door were the printed words, "HEALTER SKELTER," with helter being misspelled.

A ravelled piece of paper was found in the dining room, stained with blood and frayed on one end, indicating the paper was probably used as the instrument to print the above words. There were no obvious blood spatters located within the home, but there were traces of blood in the kitchen sink and in the rear bathroom located by the rear door.

Mrs. LaBianca's body was located on the master bedroom floor, lying face down, parallel to the bed and dresser. She had bled profusely from the many stab wounds onto the floor immediate to the body. Directly by her feet on the floor was a large blood stain leading from the torso, indicating that she had crawled approximately two feet. There were no blood spatters in the room. A pillowcase was also covering her head, with the electrical cord from one of the two toppled bedside lamps wrapped around her neck. This indicated she crawled until the electrical cord became taut, causing both the mutually-connected lamps to fall. She was attired in a nightgown and peignoir. Both the nightgown and peignoir were up over her shoulders and head, exposing her buttocks and back.

There were numerous stab wounds observable on the buttocks and back. There was no evidence of ransacking or obviously missing property. The only indication of missing property was Mrs. LaBianca's purse standing open on top of a liquor cabinet located in the dining room, and the contents appeared to be disheveled. It was later established that Mrs. LaBianca's wallet containing California driver's license and numerous credit cards was missing.

Through questioning the first police units at the scene, it was established that the east side door leading from the living room-dining room area to the outside was standing ajar. The front door was closed,

Claude L. Brown, M.D.
176 Louiselle Street
Mobile, Alabama 36607

October 22, 1970

Mr. Paul J. Fitzgerald
672 South Lafayette Park Place, Suite 38
Los Angeles, California 90057 RE: Patricia Krenwinkel

Dear Mr. Fitzgerald:

At the request and with the permission of Mr. M. A. Marsal of Mobile, I am pleased to send you the following report concerning my examination of Patricia Krenwinkel.

At the request of Mr. Marsal, I examined Miss Krenwinkel for the first and only time, for approximately two and one-half hours, in the privacy of the office of the Sheriff of Mobile County in the Mobile County Jail on December 24, 1969. She was brought into the Sheriff's office and noone else was with us during the interview. She says that she was arrested here around three weeks ago, that she had been living with a sister in Los Angeles prior to joining the Manson group but does not remember how long she was living with her sister. She says that her parents were divorced when she was about sixteen years of age, that they never got along well, rarely talked to each other. She lived with her mother for a while in Mobile after the divorce, saw her father every week or so, then moved back and forth between Mobile and California for several years. She went one semester to Spring Hill College here in Mobile, not sure of the year, perhaps 1966, was studying English "I was going to be an English teacher." A girlfriend came to visit her from California. They took an "acid trip together," and this girl asked her to return to Los Angeles which she did. She thinks that she worked in an insurance office for around six months there and lived with her sister in California. One day on the beach she met Charles Manson. She says that he played the guitar, sang, and she thought he perhaps was Jesus Christ, that at first he was very kind and gentle to her so she went to live with him for around two or three years during which time they roamed around the country. She had no contact with her family during this time.

Fig. 10a, 10b, 10c, and 10d. Patricia Krenwinkel's psychological evaluation report. Authors' collection.

2 - Continued

She says that she had taken acid twice before she met Charles, that the hallucinogenic experience produced by the acid "made things seem bright and happy - like you were a god." She usually had hallucinations for several days after having taken acid. For the first year or so that she lived with Manson she says that he told her and the other people, whom he gradually accumulated around him, that if "they did right he would take them to the center of the desert and through a hole in the ground into which Montezuma had disappeared." And presumably this journey would result intheir finding a realm of eternal tranquility. This sounded quite desirable to her. Later, Charles gained the favor of several other women more than he did Patricia and she was then relegated to such tasks as combing through garbage cans from which the group frequently ate. They traveled around the desert and finally arrested in the desert, taken to jail. She was released, then came here because of her fear of Manson. After the first year or so with Manson, she says that her feelings for him changed and she became intensely fearful of him because he became cruel to them whereas at first he was a kind benefactor; later he became the devil and threatened them with harm if they did not do what he requested. She says he "tricked many people by deluding them that he was Jesus Christ." The group never engaged in any useful occupation but says that Charles always had acid or other drugs which they all took frequently. Pertaining to the murders and in which she was allegedly involved, she gives the following story: She says that she had just come off an acid trip and was feeling bad when she was awakened by Charles, that he told her to accompany Chuck and do what was told. She, Chuck, Linda and Susan then went to a house and she says that Chuck killed the people there. She says that she did not do any of the murders. She says that Chuck shot several of the people, that Charles was not there. She says as soon as they arrived at the pace that Chuck shot one man so she, Patricia, then realized that something bad was going on. They then went into the house and he killed the other people. He asked her to help him hold the ropes. She says that she and the other girls helped him and that he told one of them to write something on the door. They did not talk much about their actions afterward "Charles said not to." They left the house, went back to the desert "I was glad to get to the desert." After they returned to the desert

3 - Continued

she was upset she says and cried, sometime later Charles told them, she says, to get in the car again with Chuck and do what he said and that again they went and killed two people. She says that she worried about the people "it'd be easier to have Charles kill me." She says she was always fearful that they would be arrested for what they had done but Charles assured them that noone could ever apprehend them. "Charles said nobody could touch us." She said she had never been to the Tate home before and knew none of the people.

She has not had any medical attention in the past several years. She says that Charles always treated them himself and did not believe in doctors. There is no history in her of any other relevant illnesses, injuries or operations except that she has had some kind of blackout spells for the past six or eight months, described by her as occasional periods of apparently syncope occuring when she stands up. These can occur either with or without ingestion of drugs. She feels dizzy afterward but then shortly feels alright. She never has injured herself in any of these spells and it is doubtful that she has actually been unconscious during these. There is no familial history of any relevant illnesses that can be elicited. She says that after she was released from the jail that she came to Mobile to live with her mother and other relatives primarily because she was exceedingly afraid of Charles finding her and killing her. She says that her flight to Alabama was motivated entirely by this fear rather than any fear of the police.

Examination revealed a thin, rather disheveled white female. She shows occasional inappropriate giggling and smiling although her emotional reactions are usually remarkably flat, and she appears quite preoccupied. She has some hair growth, more than normally seen, over her arms and chest. Her fingernails are in poor condition. Her facies is dull and preoccupied. She is quite withdrawn. "I don't feel much of anything." She walks stiffly and usually appears to be looking into a great distance. For instance, in the Sheriff's office is an aquarium and several times during the interview Patricia would interrupt the conversation, stop and admire the fish and then murmur "they just swim and play." She has almost constant auditory hallucinations

4 - Continued

she says and the subject of these hallucinations are fearful threats made by Manson. She hears him talking to her while she is conversing with me. She says that he tells her that she will never be able to get away from him, that there is no place to run or hide, that he has control of hermind and that he will kill her. She says that he never says any more kind or loving things to her any more and the content of his communication with her is threatening and fearful. Her fund of general information is adequate. She volunteers data at times and other times lapses into quietness. Her proverb interpretation is fair. Her only thought of the future is that Charles will kill her. "Nothing is going to turn out any good - everything is already ruined anyway." Although she says that she is worried about the alleged murders she also says, as indicated above, that she realizes that her emotional responses are altered and that her feelings are not entirely appropriate with her actions. "Sometimes I feel fear and sometimes I feel real happy - like maybe things are alright but then again I know they're not." She says she reads the Bible some and enjoys poetry. "I like to read fairy tales." It is noteworthy that in her history she apparently was quite fond of her father, that he and she played together and that he apparently has always been quite interested in her. They had many good times together and read fairly tales together at times.

It is my opinion that at the time I saw Miss Krenwinkel she shows a schizophrenic reaction, mixed type, with emotional flatness and withdrawal, impaired judgement, loosening of thought processes and auditory hallucinations. I do not state with any certainty that this psychosis existed at the time of the alleged murders but it is obvious that at that time she was a severely emotionally disorganized personality and probably psychotic. I think that her original poorly organized personality structure was progressively disorganized, fragmented and able to operate in very poor fashion under the influence of chronic hallucinogenic experiences plus difficult external reality situations such as a state of highly fluctuating and often fearful emotional experiences engendered by her associates

Fig. 11. Photo of the "Gypsy Shack" that Mary Neiswender was shown when she went to Spahn Ranch to talk to Charlie's girls. His phone call from jail that day cannot be explained. At that time, he wasn't supposed to use the phone. Authors' collection.

Fig. 12. Charlie's girls, sitting outside the courthouse waiting for him. *Herald Examiner* Collection.

Fig. 13. The two faces of Charlie Manson, what Mary Neiswender calls the "charming Charlie" and the darker, more solemn Charlie. Authors' collection.

Fig. 14. The original invitation to the Helter Skelter party for the press corps in October 1970, with many inside jokes hidden on it. Bugliosi even attended (although uninvited). Authors' collection.

Fig. 15. The "Hippie Murders" song sheet, a parody to come out of the Helter Skelter press party. Authors' collection.

Fig. 16. The press corps at the Helter Skelter party. Mary Neiswender is seated at the front alongside Ron Hughes, who died shortly after this photo was taken. The sheriff thought Ron Hughes was killed by Manson Family members—a hit ordered by Charlie—but there was no proof. Authors' collection.

Fig. 17. The three so-called sob sisters of the Manson trial—from left: Mary Neiswender, Theo Wilson of the *New York Daily News*, and Linda Deutsch of the Associated Press. Authors' collection.

Fig. 18. Charlie's attorney, Irving Kanarak. An engineer who had been responsible for several patents, Kanarak came late to the law. Charlie liked him as a person but hated him as a lawyer. Authors' collection.

Fig. 19. A courtroom artist's sketch of Charlie throwing away the Constitution while yelling at the judge. Even before the jury was seated, he was frustrated with the process. Authors' collection.

Fig. 20. The three defendants—Patricia Krenwinkel, Susan Atkins, and Leslie Van Houten—gave the Nazi salute to Judge Older more than once, sometimes shouting “Hail Ceasar!” They were a cold-blooded bunch, especially Atkins, who described her murder of Sharon Tate as “no big thing.” Authors’ collection.

Fig. 21. A courtroom sketch artist's rendering of the verdict. Mary Neiswender thought Charlie thought he would go free that day—he looked upbeat and smiling, but dropped into despair as the verdicts were read. Authors' collection.

Fig. 22. A gift from one of the sketch artists, signed by most of the press corps. Authors' collection.

NATIONAL BROADCASTING COMPANY, INC.

THIRTY ROCKEFELLER PLAZA, NEW YORK, N.Y. 10020, CIRCLE 7-8300

September 9, 1975

Mr. Charles Manson
San Quentin Penitentiary
San Quentin, California 94964

Dear Mr. Manson,

I am writing about the possibility of pation on NBC's Tomorrow Program. Tom night talk show on the NBC network. imately one hundred sixty cities reaches a viewing audience o We are on the air four n evening. In the past State Penitentiar program to ta last Sept two ye ou

London Daily Mirror

UNITED STATES BUREAU
220 EAST 42nd STREET, SUITE 3103
TELEPHONE: (212) 687-2686
CABLES MIRRORPIC NEW YORK
TELEX: 126713

Mirror Group Newspapers Limited
Holborn Circus London EC1P 1DQ
Switchboard: 01-353 0246
Direct Line: 01-822 3..........
Telegrams: Mirror London EC1
Telex: 27286

Anthony Delano
Chief of U.S. Bureau
wants to come

interested in

Best regards,

Pamela Burke

Pamela Burke
Associate Producer
TOMORROW

PB/pm

Fig. 23. The press continued to ask Charlie for interviews long after he was sent to prison. He sometimes asked Mary Neiswender about which ones to accept. After his years of living with the Family—who would do anything for him—Charlie was lonely. His contact with the outside world was limited to reporters. Most of his Family members were in jail or prison within a few years of his conviction. Authors' collection.

9-19-79

Dear Mary! Thanks for your letter!
#1 Kristin, my wife, and I only
do interviews together now! Also,
we have only done one with ABC
On Radar. L.A. Ch.7 Eyewitness News!
Portion of it has been on concerning our marriage 12 days ago +
another will be on in November
concerning our mission with kids
and the areas you mentioned,
but no details! I am very shy
about interviews. I have been
burnt in many negitive app-
roaches due to my past so
I have to see a positive app-
roach first from all I deal
with. I have no faith in

Train up a child in the way he should go: and when he is old, he will not depart from it.

Proverbs 22:6.

Reporters. I do have a misson
and dream. Both Kristin + I
will reach thousands of kids
for Christ, together! I wish
to downgrade Manson, take

Happy are the
Little Ones who
are in your care.
While you are
caring for them,
remember,
I Care For You!

eyes off past, + see now
what positive happenings
can occure out of this
mess for the saving of
kids who worship manson!
Kris + I will talk about involvement with you + get back
to you soon, but no details
for you now! PLEASE UNDERSTAND!
Charles

Fig. 24. A Christmas card from Tex Watson. Watson turned to Jesus after his conviction and continues to operate a Christian ministry from prison. Authors' collection.

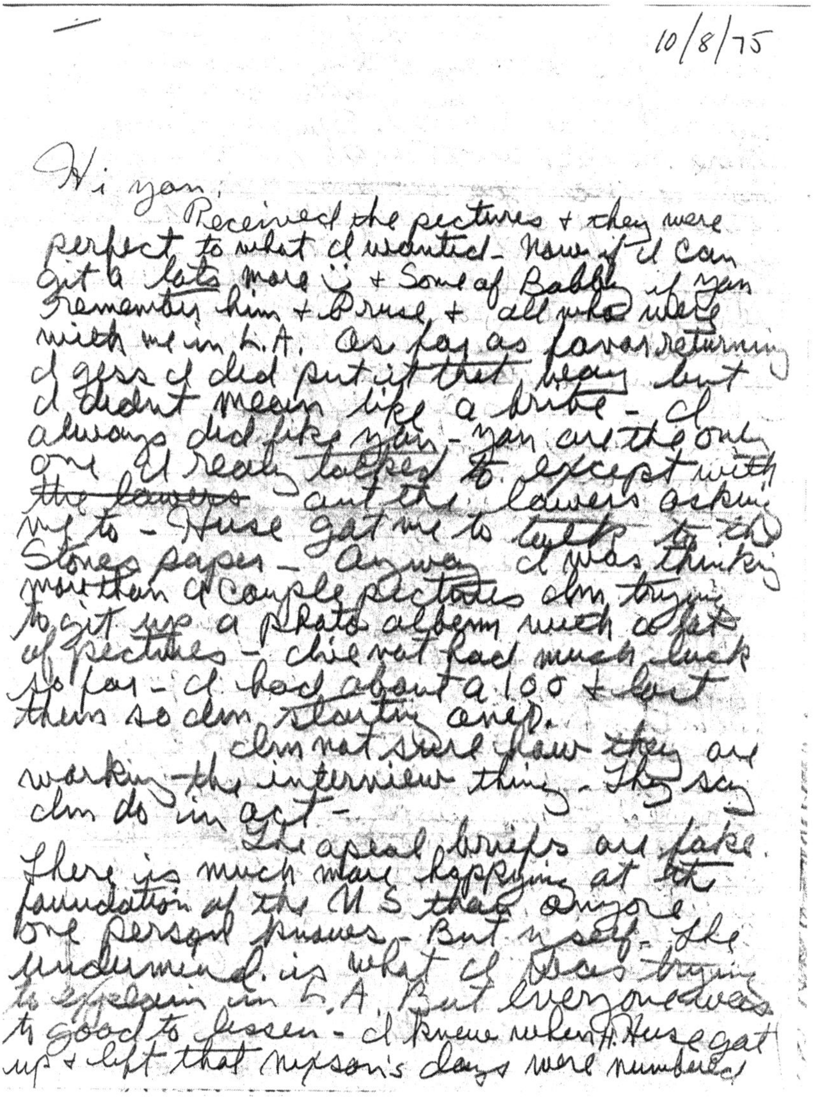

10/8/75

Hi you;
Received the pictures + they were perfect to what I wanted - now if I can get a lots more :) + some of Bobby if you remember him + Bruse + all who were with me in L.A. As far as favor returning I gess I did put it that way but I didnt mean like a bribe - I always did like you - you are the only one I really talked to except with ~~the lawers~~ and the lawers asking me to - Huse got me to talk to the Stones paper - Anyway I was thinking more than a couple pictures I'm trying to get up a photo album with a lot of pictures - I've not had much luck so far - I had about a 100 + lost them so I'm starting over.

I'm not sure how they are working - the interview thing - They say I'm do in act -

The apeal briefs are fake. There is much more happening at the foundation of the U S than anyone one person knows - But n self - The undermind is what I was trying to explain in L.A. But everyone was to good to lissen - I knew when H. Huse got up + left that Nixon's days were numbered

Fig. 25. Manson's prison letters to Mary Neiswender. Authors' collection.

6 The Press Were Part of the Story

After Charlie's arrest, three months after the 1969 murders, the global media descended upon Los Angeles, chasing headlines about a man who called himself Jesus Christ and who led a cult of killer hippies. Everyone wanted an interview, and top radio, TV, and newspaper reporters jockeyed with lawyers, judges, and police to get access. It wasn't too long before the press became part of the story.

Each time I left the jail after talking to Charlie, I felt a bit guilty. I warned him—over and over again—that I was going to print what he told me, and that if he didn't want something in print, he shouldn't tell me. But he couldn't seem to censor himself. I don't think anything I printed got to the jury, but it was Charlie himself who famously held up the banner headline proclaiming that then-President Richard Nixon thought Charlie and his girls were guilty.

It is difficult to describe the media frenzy at the Manson trial. It was the first truly global media-fueled trial. Since then, there have been several high-profile trials—OJ Simpson, Casey Anthony, and others. But the Manson trial was the first, a grand spectacle, and it was the focus of front-page stories every day for more than a year. Reporters came from all over the world to cover the trial. The coverage of the case was—by itself—a concern for the defendants.

In 1970, I had been a reporter for the Long Beach *Press-Telegram* for twenty years. I was a curiosity to my colleagues at the paper, who were still not used to a woman in the newsroom. The men wanted me relegated to covering weddings and society events. But I was a reporter of hard news, and I looked down on society coverage as ridiculous. For years, I had to fight for every story. When they played tricks on me, like putting up nude photos of men around my desk,

I put on a smile and paid them back in kind. Years of practical jokes between me and the men probably helped get me the respect I wanted.

It helped that I was raised in San Pedro, the small community at the Los Angeles waterfront. My father was a fisherman, born on a small island in the Adriatic Sea, who left Europe after the First World War. My mother joined him a few years later and worked packing tuna at the canneries. As the youngest of four children, when Mama was at the cannery, I was in charge of cooking and cleaning for the others, even at a very young age. By the time I was a teenager, I knew how to swear in a half-dozen languages, and my friends and contacts in the Longshoremen's Union often came in handy, including the time one of them helped set up my first phone call with Charlie.

I had to force the newspaper's editors to take me seriously, and I did it by bringing them stories from the rough streets of the LA waterfront. I wasn't cut out for the society pages. I wanted hard news, and I was willing to fight for it.

My parents were appalled.

My sister was a secretary. "Why don't you be a secretary like your sister?" was something I heard for years, even after I began accumulating awards for my writing. In my decades of work on the *Press-Telegram*, none of my family—not my parents, my two brothers, or my sister—subscribed to the paper. I remember my brother Andy joking with me that he would read it "later," but I don't know if "later" ever came. I was still the little sister, the youngest. The glaring headlines in huge black type over my award-winning stories were never seen by any of my family.

When I started covering the Manson trial, the one thing that stood out to me, personally, was the number of women in the national press corps. Theo Wilson was a reporter for the New York *Daily News*, a veteran of the news business. She was a few years older than me and turned out to be the ringleader of our little group. Linda Deutsch was a few years younger than me, and was covering the trial for the Associated Press, a nationwide wire service. Sandi Gibbons was working for LA's own City News Service.

Every major American news outlet had a representative at the trial, all jostling for one of only ninety-two seats in the courtroom. The international press was there as well, including two London dailies, Italy's influential *La*

Stampa, and German and French newspapers and news magazines. The TV stations covered the trial early but couldn't afford to leave their crews at the courthouse day in and day out. But when the jury started deliberations, the parking lot was jammed full of television news crews.

As for me, I walked into the Los Angeles Criminal Courts Building as a forty-three-year-old woman from a local paper. I was seen by the other reporters as too young, working for a local rag, with no "real" experience. But they couldn't get around the fact that I had access to Charlie in jail, and no one else could get in the door.

One of the country's top-tier news magazines, *Newsweek,* published an article about me on August 31, 1970. The story called me "the greatest reporter at the trial." The reporter from the LA *Free Press,* a so-called underground paper, was also praised as "colorful." The *Newsweek* article was a first for me, a national news outlet detailing many of my scoops that helped make me a big name in the business:

> The Los Angeles courtroom where Charles Manson and three members of his "family" are currently being tried for murder contains only 92 seats for spectators. More than half of them are regularly occupied by a press contingent that includes fifteen TV and radio reporters, plus representatives from five wire services, ten U.S. and four foreign dailies and three news magazines. Most of the newsmen are veteran reporters and a few of them, such as The New York *Daily News'* Theo Wilson, have made a specialty of covering murder trials. Yet, surprisingly enough, the most colorful copy on the Manson trial is being turned out by the lone representative of the underground press, and the two journalistic scoops that have so far affected the trial's course have been the work of Mary Neiswender, a relative newcomer who reports for the Ridder chain's Long Beach Independent (morning) Press-Telegram (evening). . . .
>
> Mary Neiswender, who likes to sprinkle her copy with phrases such as "accused wolfpack killer" and "accused murder marauders," is very much a "straight" reporter [as compared to the gentleman from the *Free Press*]. But her dogged digging after new leads in the case has won her

the respect not only of her colleagues but of defense attorneys. "She's right out of the '30s," says lawyer Paul Fitzgerald. "But I subscribe to the Long Beach paper so I can read her stuff."

No wonder. The defense subpoenaed Mrs. Neiswender's notes when she came up with the exclusive account of a still unidentified male neighbor of Sharon Tate who heard "a loud shot, a woman's scream, then another shot, more muffled [at] 2 or 2:30—no earlier" on the morning of Aug. 9, 1969. Since all other evidence places the time of the murders at about 12:15 a.m., the defense has desperately tried to find Mrs. Neiswender's source in order to raise a reasonable doubt about the validity of the state's case. "I promised to protect the man," says Mrs. Neiswender, a suburban mother of two, in her best PTA chairman's voice, and her paper says the notes were "destroyed in the ordinary course of business."

Both the defense and the prosecution have also been unable to find the source of another Neiswender exclusive. Last spring, in an anonymous article in the Harvard Crimson, a student related he had hitchhiked from California to New Mexico with Linda Kasabian shortly after the murders. Mrs. Neiswender tracked down the author, James Breckenridge of Dallas, and in a phone interview he told her Linda had mentioned a "great secret" (which might support the prosecution's case) but also praised Manson family members for their "spirit of lovemaking" (which could help the defense). Breckenridge said he would come to Los Angeles if Mrs. Neiswender could get him into court.

Mrs. Neiswender got Breckenridge a second row seat, from which the 6-foot, 6-inch young man watched Mrs. Kasabian undergo a tough cross-examination. After talking with Mrs. Kasabian's attorney, Breckenridge told Mrs. Neiswender, "I'm splitting," and promptly left. The police searched for him to no avail, and the defense and prosecution alike demanded to know why Mrs. Neiswender had not identified the visitor. "It's not part of my job," she said. "The defense knew I'd written the story and saw the kid fitting the description in court."

For a while, too, Mrs. Neiswender seemed to have an inside track to Charlie Manson himself, who granted her ten telephone or face-to-face

> interviews. But after Breckenridge's appearance in court, Manson turned his formidable gaze upon Mrs. Neiswender and made a quick motion across his throat with a forefinger. Since then, she has received several after-midnight telephone calls at home, and each time there has been no voice at the other end.

The Breckenridge incident mentioned in this story was quite a coup. When Linda Kasabian left California after the murders, she headed east. In her testimony to the district attorney, she claims she was frightened, but James Breckenridge says he traveled with her through New Mexico, and she wasn't frightened at all—though he described her as "kind of possessed."

Breckenridge says Kasabian picked him up in what she claimed was her father's car. But that was certainly not true, and Breckenridge said he figured that out when the credit cards in the car didn't work. They traveled together for only twenty-four hours, with Breckenridge leaving Kasabian in Taos, New Mexico. Breckenridge explained to me on the phone: "She mentioned Charlie of course—and called him the devil. She said he was definitely the leader of the group—the guiding face—but was a non-leader. Charlie was the guy, she said, who listened to 'Helter Skelter' and got the subliminal message from the Beatles. She talked of the hole in the earth and Helter Skelter and getting ready for the race war."

Kasabian's story was how Vince Bugliosi came up with the "Helter Skelter" theory for the Tate murders. Apparently, after the war with the Blacks, which the Blacks would win, the Family would survive in a hole in the desert. There was also talk about the hole being the location of Montezuma, the great Aztec emperor. Charlie didn't talk to me about this angle and I'm not sure that Kasabian didn't make the whole thing up.

Kasabian said nothing to Breckenridge about being afraid, but he was convinced something was driving her: "It showed up in how excited she was—how eagerly she let me in on secrets." But the "secrets" were general stuff, nothing specific.

"When I met her in Gallup, she struck me as really kind of possessed," Breckenridge said. "Something was really making her go. She was being moved by something very powerful. I knew she had something going on. I took a special interest in her because she was very evangelical. She seemed to be saying, 'I know something you ought to know, and I'd love to tell you about it.' But she didn't."

Kasabian's car broke down, and since the credit cards didn't work, Kasabian and Breckenridge hitchhiked together from Albuquerque to Taos. It was during this leg of their journey that Kasabian told Breckenridge about her baby—which she had left with the Family—and said she "had given the baby back to itself." She claimed she was looking for her husband.

Breckenridge's story was printed anonymously in Harvard University's *Crimson*, the college newspaper. It took a lot of phone calls, and pulling in some favors, to get his name and then his phone number, but after I published the story about Breckenridge and Kasabian, both the prosecution and the defense teams were all over me. They wanted his contact information, and I said "no." First, I said "no" politely, but things became more and more heated, with Bugliosi threatening me with jail for contempt and the defense claiming I was working for the prosecution. Even Charlie was upset with me over this.

After that, one of the most unsettling incidents happened at my home. It was a sunny southern California afternoon, and my teenage son was home. My house was a good two miles from the nearest public road, in a gated community. Two hippies—a man and a woman, both in their early twenties—showed up at my front door. Because it was the middle of the afternoon, I wasn't home. They asked my son for a match. He was smart enough not to let them in the house, but he talked to them for a while, and he gave them a book of matches. They were pleasant, but he thought it was very strange. The only thing he could think of was that they wanted to get high and were out of matches. He told me they smiled and talked about nothing important, and he didn't feel threatened. But he didn't let them in the house. I knew it was a message, direct from Charlie. He was telling me he could find me, he could find my children. It didn't change my writing, but it was unsettling to say the least.

The thought of my fifteen-year-old son coming face to face with some of Charlie's Family turned my stomach. I went straight to the jail and yelled at Charlie. I trusted him at this point, and I told him, "What the hell did you think you were doing, sending people to my house. How can I trust you if you screw up like that?"

He said it wouldn't happen again, and it didn't. But it damaged our relationship for a long time. The not-so-subtle threat to my family didn't matter though—the trial was the center of the universe as far as the media was concerned and nothing could keep me away. Nothing compared to the visit from Charlie's Family members for years, until I started working on organized crime connections to a scandal in the city of Long Beach. There were threats then as well, and I am pretty sure that a "stray" bullet that hit a plate glass window at my house was another threat, another "stay away from the story" moment.

But I knew about Charlie's control over his Family, and I knew all too well how dangerous they could be. They could have killed my son. Nothing compares to that feeling.

At one point, I took my son with me to a hearing at the courthouse before the trial. My son was a tall kid, over six feet in height and an athlete, so he had a good ten inches over Charlie's small stature. When he left the courtroom, my son kept asking me, "Was that really Charlie Manson?" He couldn't believe that Charlie could have done what was in all the papers. Charlie impressed my son as being so small and slender that he couldn't possibly be a threat. I didn't try to explain to him that Charlie used others . . . just as he had sent the two hippies to my front door.

Charlie was very aware of the media frenzy surrounding his case. In June 1970, jury selection had just begun, and Charlie complained that "they're turning all the honest people away—and leaving the dishonest ones": "I sit in there and listen to their questions—especially about the publicity and whether they've made up their minds about me. Most of them say 'no, no, I haven't really—no, no, I haven't made up my mind' and they let them stay in the jury. A couple have said 'yah, I read it all and think he's guilty' and they let them out. They're turning all the honest people away and leaving the dishonest ones. I'd rather have the honest ones, even though they said they were influenced by the publicity."

Charlie told me that people have been "mesmerized" by the media and his case has been hurt by the "prosecution trying the case in the press." He told me the press people in the courtroom ". . . all look like intelligent people sitting out there taking notes, but they must be stupid. How could they be so blind? What kind of system is this?"

"If someone came into the courtroom and blew my brains out it wouldn't make any difference. All they'd lose is one small guy—they're not losing much. But what the people are doing is destroying themselves."

Jury selection took more than a month. In all 141 people were examined. Ten times, the defense team accepted the jury "as constituted," while the prosecution systematically eliminated all members of minority groups—Latinos, Blacks, and Jews. Only one Latino remained on the panel, which included two ex-policemen, a social worker, a mortician, and several housewives. One woman was a former member of the Los Angeles Sheriff's Department. Another juror had a brother who was a reserve deputy sheriff.

And this was just for the first twelve jurors. It started all over again for the six alternates. Seventy-three potential jurors were examined before the six alternates were chosen. Attorney Ron Hughes called the jury a "tragedy," saying the jury didn't represent the community: "We had to accept those that could be sequestered for six months, those that claimed they were not affected by pre-trial publicity, those who could afford to serve, and only those who believe in the death penalty." Charlie and Hughes were in sync on this. Charlie told me, "Here are twelve lying jurors, who all say they never heard of me or Sharon Tate or the murders. You believe that?"

At this point, before the jury was seated in July 1970, Charlie was already creating theater out of the proceedings. He would stand in court and turn his back on the judge, or spread his arms and stand as if he were crucified. The press lapped it up.

Charlie had a thoughtful explanation for his antics: "If you stand for it (the system) you are part of it. I've looked at the judge and looked at him, but he won't look at me, so I don't think of him anymore. I see a black robe, the same one Pilate wore. It's got all the blood on it from 1900 years of Christian rule." Not for the first or last time, he talked about representing himself: "If I were my own attorney I could explain. You've heard of the Battle of Armageddon (the Bible's prophecy of the last decisive battle between good and evil). I see it coming and all I want to do is get out of the way, but they're trying to stick an antichrist label on me."

Thoughtful or not, the antics went on inside and outside of the courtroom daily. And we loved it. But it was exhausting. I would get up in the morning, and call into the paper to update the lede and the story for the morning editions. Then off to the courthouse for the morning session. At the noon break, all the reporters would scramble to the press room or crowd around the pay phones to call in stories for the afternoon editions. Remember, there were no computers, no cell phones, no communications equipment other than pay phones.

At the end of the day, we would again run to the phones or get in the car to get back to the office to file stories for the evening editions. In 1970, my paper had five daily editions, and each edition wanted a fresh lede and updated facts. If I had any time at all, I would run to the jail and get Charlie's take on the day's proceedings. And I did this every day, five days a week. We all did, all the reporters covering the trial.

The press corps could be cruel. I have reviewed some of the published descriptions of the jurors. In one story (not mine), a woman juror was described as "hefty," and another as "red-faced." I remember one being given the nickname of "Mrs. Eichmann" for her ice-cold stare and white gloves (which wasn't used in print). One man was described as a "bespectacled preacher-type." Another sat so still in the jury box that the press speculated as to whether he had died.

Probably the worst description was saying one woman had a "drooping lower lip" with "midriff bulges." It didn't help that her husband went on television during the jury's deliberations to say she had become "argumentative, prone to hysterics, and a drinker." The press loved that. Even worse for the poor woman, Charlie's lawyer, Irving Kanarek, brought a motion to have her dismissed as a juror, claiming she had been "mentally affected" by the tight security and sensational publicity surrounding the trial. Kanarek wanted her dismissed because she was "not capable of rendering a decision" in the case. This was strange because the jury had just come back with a guilty verdict the week before. Kanarek wanted her off the penalty phase of the trial.

I met some reporters that became friends, and we stayed friends for years. Theo Wilson was a well-known crime reporter from the New York *Daily News*.

She was a marvel, a small woman with a quick smile and an ability to laugh that still makes me smile.

One day at trial, there were the four of us sitting in the front row of the press section. It was Linda Deutsch, Sandi Gibbons, Theo, and me. We were passing notes like high school kids, and Theo starting giggling. One of the notes had made her laugh and she couldn't stop. So she stood up, barely keeping it under control, stepped over to the aisle and stepped smack into a metal trashcan. At that point, she gasped with laughter and couldn't stop. She ran out the door. Of course, when that happened, none of us could stop laughing and we all stumbled into the aisle and out of the courtroom.

Vince Bugliosi stared daggers at us. He already hated us. This didn't help. I understand he called us the "sob sisters" in print. To our faces, he was much cruder.

We decided that we should have a huge party, a big blowout before the end of trial, when all our trial friends would fly back to all corners of the earth. Besides, we had all worked very long hours, and the trial had been extremely gruesome at times. We needed a party, and a chance to play. We had flyers printed and called it our "Helter Skelter" party.

Charlie knew about the party, of course. In the courtroom shortly before the party, he turned to the press corps and told us all, "When I get out of here, I'm going to give a real Helter Skelter party and you're all invited."

We arranged for rental of a hotel suite. Everyone was told to come in costume, and almost everyone did. Reporters from prestigious publications had red *X*'s painted onto their foreheads, matching the one Charlie had carved into his own forehead. All were in hippie dress, some daubed in fake blood.

There was a golden rope, attached to the ceiling and going down into the toilet, a reference to one of the Family members saying he was going to climb down a golden rope to the bottomless pit, hence the toilet.

The party was an invitation-only affair, but word spread fast. No one would admit to inviting Vince Bugliosi, but he showed up anyway, along with dozens of others, some I don't think were part of the press corps or even associated with the trial. It was a great party.

There was some fallout. A rumor spread that the beautiful downtown hotel where we had hosted the party had let in actual Family members. Apparently, our costumes had been more believable than we thought. Certainly, our behavior had not met with the well-behaved standards our newspapers generally demanded of us.

At the end of it, most of us were not sober. We tried to get cabs for the worst of the tipsy reporters, but some of them ended up passed out in the underground parking garage. There were tire marks in the garage the next day—someone, and we know it was one of us, had driven donuts, leaving huge skid mark circles.

Thank God it happened on a Friday. We never would have made it to court the next day.

The press was given preferential seating, with rows and rows of seating reserved for reporters, instead of the general public. That, too, became an issue later in the case: in January 1971, the defense filed a motion for a mistrial, claiming that a fair trial was made impossible because the public was essentially denied access to the trial. This certainly fit into the arguments made by Charlie's attorney, who argued that Charlie was being tried in the press, not in the courtroom.

One of the strangest stories I wrote about the case—and there were quite a few—was published right after the murders in the fall of 1969. I was scrambling to find something, anything, that was new and that wasn't already part of the story for reporters everywhere. So my paper sent me back to the neighborhood. A friend of mine, Chris, and I tried to get onto the Tate property, but it was well guarded, so we found neighbors to talk to. One of them heard screams and gunshots and set a time for the murder. The police hadn't even talked to him yet. But Chris and I were running out of material, so Chris suggested that I talk to Joseph DeLouise, a Chicago-based psychic, born in Sicily and with a good record of predicting things, like train crashes and the collapse of a bridge in West Virginia.

I was an unbeliever, skeptical as could be. But, less than two weeks after the Tate-LaBianca murders, I was on the phone with DeLouise. I wrote:

> The yet unsolved murder of movie star Sharon Tate and four others in her Benedict Canyon home was the work of "thrill killers," a nationally-known Chicago psychic claims.
>
> "This was a thrill murder . . . their joy was killing. . . . they have no conscience . . . They don't feel sorry about it . . . Three people committed the crime . . . one weighs 160 pounds with darkish blonde hair. . . . the other is shorter with dark hair. . . . One of the suspects could be in Texas. . . . one is a girl named Linda. She's a runaway on drugs."

DeLouise went on to say that both the Tate killings and the LaBianca murders were committed by the same group. This was at a time that Los Angeles police were certain the LaBianca killings were a "copycat" of the Tate killings, and completely unrelated. The chief of police claimed the killers had "randomly" selected the Tate home for the killing spree. DeLouise said the Tate house was targeted.

DeLouise intuited that the murder was done by "script," meaning that it was planned. He said there were three killers and there were drugs involved. He said that five people would be indicted, but the rest may be associated with the crime as witnesses, knowing about it, but not participating. In retrospect, that seemed pretty close. He said he was positive there was something about money—some money that wasn't exchanged. I thought about Charlie's record contract, promised but not received. Late in the trial, there was testimony about $5,000 that Kasabian stole for Charlie, but never gave to him. DeLouise also said a small van or truck was used and police verified that a small panel truck was used in the crimes.

DeLouise made some claims that didn't pan out as well. He said it would be "almost impossible to bring these people to trial. There are no witnesses. . . . One will be freed, the other two tied up in court but never really prosecuted for the crime." He said there was a woman with a cat who was not telling all she knows—hard to say if that was accurate.

DeLouise also said a big break in the case would happen in September, specifically September 14 and 15. I didn't know for months, but DeLouise was spot on: that's the date when Inyo County authorities first ran into members of the Manson clan, some of whom were arrested a few weeks later, with sheriff's deputies thinking they were car thieves. One of Charlie's followers broke under questioning, saying her boyfriend, Bobby Beausoleil, and Sadie Atkins were involved in the Hinman killing.

At that point, the deputies had a lot more on their hands than some missing cars.

I wrote the DeLouise story in August 1969, and thought nothing more about it for months. When a warrant was issued for Tex Watson, a blonde man from Texas weighing 156 pounds, I remembered DeLouise's predictions. At the same time, a warrant was issued for Charlie, described as a short man with dark hair. DeLouise was right about so much: the link between the Tate and LaBianca killings, the date of the "big break" when members of the Family were arrested in Inyo County, even descriptions of the people involved. And "Linda the runaway" could have been Linda Kasabian. DeLouise said five people would be indicted and five were: Charlie, Tex Watson, and the three girls.

After my story ran, DeLouise told me he started to get threatening calls, about twenty in all. He was threatened, as was his family. He lived in Chicago, two thousand miles away. Fortunately, nothing happened to DeLouise.

Joseph DeLouise was a great interview and his predictions were uncanny. Still, to this day, I don't place much faith in crime psychics. But he knew so much before the police did. You have to wonder.

Even after the convictions, when Charlie and his girls were in prison, the press continued to write to Charlie, asking for interviews. Charlie sent them all to me, asking if he should do one or the other, and urging me to come see him. In his letters, Charlie's feelings towards me were still positive. He wrote: "I love the truth—you are one of the few people who were always truthful with me. Be true with me and I'm with you as your servant." I always warned him that I was going to write the story as I saw it, and he respected that.

Charlie told me he was messing with the reporters, telling some lies, some the truth. I'm sure he went into his "you are me and I am you" routine. That was standard fare. But when I read the interviews published both in the United

States and around the world, I could tell that Charlie was having a good time, back in the spotlight, able to talk about his philosophy.

That same philosophy had resulted in the gathering of his Family. Now, he was alone, and that must have been tough.

7 The Defense of Charles Manson

It was clear from the start that Charlie was being treated differently than other prisoners and being punished for what I would call "normal" behavior. At this point—the first part of 1970—Charlie was representing himself. The judge gave him the right to three calls a day, but then cut off all phone privileges because a San Francisco radio station called the "pro per" (self-represented) module in the jail, and Charlie talked to them. Charlie told the judge, "They called me—I didn't call them." But the judge suspended his phone rights. Another time, Charlie was thrown into solitary confinement for five days for refusing to go to breakfast.

Around the same time, the judge cut off all Charlie's mail, which Charlie said made it impossible to work on his defense. No phone calls, no mail; one of Charlie's fellow prisoners said he personally witnessed guards tossing Charlie's mail in the trash. He told me, "They're really giving him a rough time." In jail, and later in prison, guards would go out of their way to be mean to Charlie. It seemed he was "fair game" and no one would help.

Charlie's jail mate also told me that Charlie's personality was changing: "They take him to the medical dispensary twice a day now, and I don't know what they're doing to him, but everybody is noticing a change in him—he's depressed, different."

Charlie's initial fear in jail was that he would "be like Jack Ruby—they shot him full of leukemia." Clearly that didn't happen—for a lifer, Charlie lived to a ripe old age, dying at the age of eighty-three. In these early months of his incarceration, he was thinking not only about putting together his defense, but dreamily remembering his time in Haight-Ashbury and how happy he was there: "I made it to Haight Ashbury and man! All those beautiful people there. There was no rejection, just plain acceptance of me—as I was, for what I was. Instead of smallness, meanness and rejection, I found love, and I loved those people there. No one cared it my hair was longer than theirs or I didn't dress like they did. It didn't make any difference, because all of them dig each other, love each other. There's no stigma because we're different."

Before trial started, Charlie and the girls stood up in the courtroom, made themselves into living signs of the cross, and screamed out: "Can't you see who we are?"

Eighty-four prosecution witnesses, thirty-two weeks of trial, and multiple murder convictions later, no one was really sure.

The prosecutor, Vince Bugliosi, argued Charlie was a master puppeteer who directed his "blood thirsty robots" to kill Sharon Tate, the LaBiancas, and the others in the summer of 1969. The average "man on the street" thought Charlie a killer who should have been hanged when he was arrested.

The girls in Charlie's Family—sitting patiently outside the Hall of Justice every day—told me and others that he was their "father," and they would sit on their street corner until he was free.

Charlie himself repeatedly said that he was society's reject—"one of your garbage people"—who took youngsters into his Family because they had no other place to go. He wanted to act as his own lawyer but was not allowed to do so. Three others would come in to provide a defense for Charlie, but he was never happy with how his defense was being handled.

As the days and weeks and months of trial dragged on, Charlie knew it was not what the world felt about him that was important, but what was in the heads of the seven men and five women who sat in judgment upon him. The answer came on January 25, 1971.

"We the jury find . . ." was how the reading of the verdict began, and Charles Manson, Susan Atkins, Patricia Krenwinkel, and Leslie Van Houten were found guilty of first-degree murder and conspiracy to commit murder in connection with the deaths of Sharon Tate, Abigail Folger, Voytek Frykowski, Jay Sebring, Steven Parent, Leno LaBianca, and Rosemary LaBianca.

What happened in those eight months in between the mock crucifixion and the verdict can be summed up in two words: fouled up.

As murder cases went, this was far from simple—multiple killings, multiple defendants, multiple attorneys, a judge who had only been on the bench for two years, and the whole thing wrapped in a lifestyle that was incomprehensible to the middle-class American jury. More than incomprehensible—it was dangerous, scary, and just plain weird.

There were a few added attractions—prosecution witnesses who dropped acid like little kids eat candy; President Nixon joining the fray and saying Charlie was guilty, "directly or indirectly"; more murder indictments during the trial; street corner surrenders; musical chair games for attorneys and for the defendants themselves.

But the antics of the attorneys in the case is a story in itself, and almost as weird as the case itself.

It started even before the trial began as Charlie switched attorneys, searching for someone who would let him control his own defense. It ended with the disappearance and death of defense attorney Ronald Hughes only days before the case went to the jury.

Charlie started out with a public defender from the small desert county of Inyo, where he and members of his tribe had been picked up in a giant raid on the Family's hideout in the heart of California's Death Valley. He was charged with stealing cars and was defended by one of the county's assigned attorneys. Before the case could get to the courts, Charlie was charged with the seven Tate-LaBianca murders and brought the Inyo County public defender with him. But the public defender didn't last long.

Charlie wanted to be his own attorney and told the court he had spent most of his life in jail because of attorneys. The judge appointed Joe Ball, a well-known and highly respected California trial lawyer who probably was best known for his role as senior counsel on the Warren Commission that investigated the assassination of President John F. Kennedy. Ball was tasked with talking to Charlie to determine whether he was capable of defending himself. Ball gave Charlie's "pro per" representation the green light. Charlie liked Ball, and Ball liked Charlie. "For an older guy," Charlie said, "he's alright."

Charlie was then allowed to begin using the jail library and the jail telephone—ostensibly for interviews. It was about this point that I had my first conversation with Charlie, with him crouched under the law library table. But he was spending little, if any, time on necessary legal motions. For a person charged with mass murder, he didn't seem worried.

The "pro per" section of the county jail was overcrowded and noisy; "pro pers" are inmates who represent themselves in court. Charlie said it was impossible to get work done, due to conditions and restrictions imposed by his jailers. He described the scene in the law library as "wall-to-wall attorneys," with the inmates working elbow-to-elbow, and the constant noise of inmates talking. Charlie must have had some respect for the other inmates, because in January 1970, Charlie asked the judge to allow him to represent himself, along with "fellow guests of the sheriff" who could help with drafting motions.

Judge George Dell called the motion "one of the strangest I've ever read," and denied it, but he was trying to work with Charlie. At one point during the hearing, the judge reminded Charlie that the prosecution was cooperating very well in his request for aid—including a defense investigator at public expense.

Charlie responded by laughing, stroking his beard, and saying, "I was just going to ask them to call the whole thing off." The press corps laughed out loud, and even the judge was smiling. Again, Charlie could be charming.

Joking or not, Charlie's anger often bubbled to the surface. He was clearly frustrated and angry with the jailhouse restrictions.

"Like the phone," he snapped at me:

> Who ever heard of a one-way setup like this one? I can phone out but no one can phone in to me! Can you imagine a district attorney or lawyer being allowed to make only three ten-minute outgoing phone calls a day, and receive no incoming calls at all? It's crazy! I am—we pro pers are—restricted as to how much and when we can defend ourselves. What if an important witness wants to call and talk to me? He can't! But the DA's witnesses can call and talk to him. That leaves him with an advantage over me.

Joe Ball may have said that Charlie was capable of defending himself, but Ball may not have known that the restrictions put on pro pers made such a defense very difficult. "I have got to have two-way phone privileges, call in and calls out. I should have the same tools as the prosecution, who have unlimited use of the telephone, not just three ten-minute calls per day."

On the subject of witnesses, Charlie was equally seething. Witness interviews were limited in duration, and the hours of the day during which they could be conducted. The rules set forth by the Superior Court limited any witness interviews to between 9:00 a.m. and 9:00 p.m. The initial interview could be longer, but any subsequent interviews were limited to thirty minutes. And Charlie told me his witnesses were badly harassed: "You know what they've been doing to my witnesses? They photograph and harass them when they come to confer with me. The DA's witnesses are not subjected to all that. . . . only mine are!" He said his Family members were being targeted:

> My witnesses are all scared and some are in jail. All of these people have had the stuffing scared out of them already. They're hiding out with the children because the juvenile authorities say, "You're not fit to be a mother." This is the kind of thing they [prosecutors] have been pulling. They take the people's child and say, "well, you're not fit to be a mother and you have to go to juvenile court." When they go to juvenile court, they have to have a lawyer and we don't have any money.
>
> One of the girls they questioned—there were fifteen girls that they arrested in Inyo and they kept some of them in solitary confinement—went to mental institution because of the interrogation they put her through. They kept the girls down there for two months and every day the LAPD would come down with the best professional men they have. They arrested them all, brought them in and scared them all to death about murder. They were just frightened to death and most of them just ran away after that.
>
> Now they have one witness of mine arrested on a phony charge, and they have an impossible bail on him and they're moving him from cell to cell. Another one they've taken to Independence [in Inyo County] and

> every time we send someone to Independence they move him to Lone Pine [fifteen miles south]. They've got three witnesses locked up there. They're applying every bit of pressure they can.
>
> They've taken one girl's baby at least three times. It really is a pretty sinister thing. But it hasn't just started, it's been going on. They blind the public. They control the publicity. They only leak out what they want you to hear. They won't leak out that they went to talk to thirty people and the thirty people said I wasn't a bad guy at all.

Charlie added that along with harassing his witnesses, inside the jail and out, when a witness came to the jail to speak with him, Charlie was strip-searched every time: "Seems like an awful lot of time is spent taking off your clothes and putting them back on again, off and on, time better spent working on your case. . . ."

His actual time at the law library was also limited. He could use the library—with the forty other pro per inmates—from 9:00 a.m. to 11:00 a.m., then from 1:00 p.m. to 3:00 p.m., and from 6:00 p.m. to 9:00 p.m. Charlie said the library should be open from early morning until late at night, without interruption. But Charlie couldn't type, and he needed to file motions with the court, so he reached out to others to help.

It didn't take long before a bunch of zany motions came out of the law library as the jailhouse lawyers and publicity-seeking attorneys tried to "help" Charlie. They helped him in only one way: they got him dumped as his own attorney.

Charlie complained and complained throughout the trial, but his objections did him no good. In one of his early motions, he asked to move his case to another county. The judge said "no." He asked for a three-to-four-year continuance, to allow time for the publicity surrounding the murders to ebb. That also brought a quick "no" from the judge.

"No one can speak for me," Charlie told me many times, and he repeated that mantra often in front of the judges of the Los Angeles County Criminal Courts. Not one of them listened to him.

In March 1970, Charlie was in court in front of Judge William Keene, arguing he had a right to represent himself. The whole thing went very badly for

Charlie. At one point, Charlie shouted, "you can kill me, but you can't give me an attorney." The wild court session grew wilder as Charlie and Judge Keene tried to out-shout each other. Judge Keene had sharply criticized a motion filed by Charlie, but Charlie hadn't written it. The motion had asked that the district attorney be incarcerated, and that Manson be released in order to travel anywhere he deemed necessary in the preparation of his defense. The judge said: "Based on your performance, I am satisfied you cannot act as your own attorney. . . . It looks like you've turned into a messenger boy, bringing in motions prepared by others."

Charlie tried to respond: "I can't deny what you say, but again, I ask the court to look through my eyes. You've given me three weeks to become an attorney. I've asked for associate counsel. I told you I couldn't be a lawyer, but I didn't want to lose my voice." At this point, Judge Keene tried to interrupt, and Charlie shouted, "Now wait a minute!"

Judge Keene began to speak louder, telling Charlie to keep quiet, but Charlie countered: "I kept quiet for you . . . now let me finish. I am a man too, mister." He had entered the courtroom smiling, but now he was almost in tears: "There's no love in your courtroom. Go wash your hands. They're dirty."

Four of Charlie's Family were sitting in the courtroom, and they jumped to their feet and started shouting their support. Deputies surrounded them, and they were arrested and taken out of the courtroom.

None of this affected Judge Keene's decision to appoint Charles Hollopeter, a defense attorney with a phenomenal record for getting people out of jail. Hollopeter thought Charlie was insane and wanted psychiatrists to back him up. Charlie disagreed. Hollopeter lasted eight days.

Just a few weeks before this exchange between Judge Keene and Charlie, Judge Keene attended an installation dinner for the Los Angeles Criminal Court Bar Association. At that dinner, a comedy skit was performed by members of the Bar Association, entitled "A Family That Slays Together, Stays Together." The singing quartet spoofed the Tate-LaBianca murders and Charlie himself. According to a man named Robert Levy, who allegedly attended the dinner, the skit "mocked Mr. Manson" and was "widely applauded" by the attendees, including Judge Keene, who—at the time—was the judge in charge of the Manson case. Mr. Levy filed a petition with the California Courts of Appeal, saying a "fair trial" had been reduced to a "farce and a sham" by the skit. Nevertheless, Judge Keene stayed on the case a little longer, faring better than the revolving door of Charlie's defense lawyers.

After Hollopeter, Charlie then hired Ronald Hughes, only a year out of law school, a portly, bearded, balding attorney who had never tried a case. Hughes would do what Charlie wanted. Again, Judge Keene was there to oversee the substitution, with Hollopeter being fired, and Hughes being brought on. During a sharp exchange between Judge Keene and Hughes, Charlie rose to his feet, saying he was being forced to accept Ron Hughes. He then held up a copy of the Constitution, saying, "but here is your Constitution." He then walked up to the bench and threw the book into the wastebasket, adding, "I was going to throw it at you but I thought I might hit you and I don't want to do that."

Hughes should have a been a good fit for Charlie. After the selection of a very white jury, Hughes told me: "We would have been very happy to go to the middle of Watts and take the first twelve people we came across. [At the time, Watts was an overwhelmingly Black community.] The prosecution purposefully threw off the Blacks and Chicanos. This is indicative of the type of treatment these people suffer under this establishment—they are thrown off everything—and Manson is an outcast of society." Charlie liked that, but it didn't save Hughes's job.

Hughes lasted just long enough for Charlie to realize he wasn't wise in the ways of law, so Charlie substituted attorneys again—this time hiring Irving Kanarek, a lawyer with a reputation for turning a week-long trial into a year-long trial.

Kanarek came to the law as a second choice. He graduated with a degree in chemical engineering from the University of Washington. He worked for eight years with North American Aviation in chemical propulsion research. Some of the things he invented were patented. Kanarek said he always wanted to go into patent law. But there he was at the counsel table, trying to keep up with a client who wanted him gone, defending the leading suspect in the most notorious murder case in recent history.

When Kanarek was hired, everybody moaned, except Charlie, who said if he couldn't be his own attorney he would get the "worst attorney" he could find. Irving Kanarek quickly interpreted his client's words to the press: "He meant 'worst' for the prosecution."

The prosecution screamed and the then-district attorney of Los Angeles County—Evelle Younger—committed one of the many publicity-seeking faux pas connected with the case. He had his "boys"—co-prosecutors Aaron Stovitz and Vince Bugliosi—challenge the competency of Kanarek before novice judge Charles Older. Novice or not, Judge Older reminded the district attorney (who was angling for higher office) that he had no jurisdiction.

Despite losing the motion, Younger didn't stop there, and in a hastily called press conference, he said he was taking the matter to the California Supreme Court. He was requesting, he said, that the high court order Judge Older to conduct a hearing on Kanarek's competence to avoid any later appeal by Manson that he was not adequately represented.

Younger was criticized by members of the legal profession for the move because the trial was in progress. Nevertheless, Younger got what he wanted: newspaper and television coverage during his campaign for California attorney general.

Although Younger said he was prepared to present testimony from eight judges that Kanarek had a "reputation for grossly obstructionist and dilatory tactics," the Supreme Court wouldn't listen.

Kanarek, with a smile and his rumpled suit, came to court.

The rumpled suit lasted, but the smile faded a few days later when Charlie tried to fire him. Charlie didn't get his way and Kanarek stayed to the end—despite Charlie's repeated attempts to fire him, and even, at one point, when Charlie, armed with a sharp pencil, threatened that if he didn't "shut up and sit down" he'd jab the pencil into Kanarek's ribs.

Charlie harassed Kanarek through the trial and into the penalty phase. It was a constant battle. I think Kanarek did the best job he could. But I have to wonder if a top-notch defense attorney—like Bill Charvet or Johnnie Cochran—could have gotten Charlie free. Other than Linda Kasabian's highly questionable ramblings, there was no testimony that put Charlie at the scene of the Tate or

LaBianca killings. The girls changed their testimony more than once but kept coming back to "Charlie never told us to kill anyone." He might have been convicted for the murder of Gary Hinman—he was there, or so said Mary Brunner—although Bobby Beausoleil did the actual killing. But the evidence pointed to the Tate-LaBianca killings being done without Charlie present.

During the penalty phase, Kanarek cross-examined the girls relentlessly, trying to get the jury to see that because Charlie wasn't there, Charlie couldn't be held responsible for the murders. The jury didn't buy it.

Kanarek may have been fired more often than the other defense attorneys, but they didn't fare well either.

Ira Reiner, a former Los Angeles prosecutor who represented Leslie Van Houten—the girl who had only two of the seven murders charged to her—was fired before jury selection was complete. His replacement was Ron Hughes, the lawyer that Charlie had fired only a few weeks before.

But Reiner, fired because he wouldn't obey his client's orders to "stand mute and offer no defense," left the case legally screaming. The young bull-voiced attorney asked that the district attorney be cited for contempt because he had knowledge of the impending publication of a "confession" by prosecution witness and Manson Family member Sadie Atkins, and Reiner said the DA was doing nothing to prevent it.

Evelle Younger basically confessed the truth of that allegation. In a letter to the judge, Younger said his part in the publication of the confession was "explainable," indicating that at least some of the charges made by Reiner were true. Nonetheless, the contempt charge was never acted upon and Younger moved onto greener pastures in California's state capital, taking with him only the judge's comment that the DA was "irresponsible."

Reiner refused to stop at citing Younger, and also rebuked the judge for misconduct because he claimed Judge Older leveled a slurring remark at him.

When the smoke cleared, Reiner was gone.

In his place, Ron Hughes was back. Hughes was potbellied, easygoing, and the closest thing to a flower child the Family could have hoped for. When he entered the case—shy, unassuming, and wide-eyed—he owned one suit and he stopped the trial dead in the water early when he once appeared without a suit coat. The judge, high on decorum but low on criminal law, refused to allow the trial to proceed—even in chambers—if all the attorneys were not wearing coats and ties.

The stalemate ended when *Newsweek* reporter Martin Kasindorf, exempt from the judge's dress code, gave his jacket to Hughes. Marty was so much smaller than Ron Hughes that the sleeves were way up on his arms when he put it on. Again, the press was part of the story.

Hughes slowly turned into a clothes horse. To avoid future problems with the judge, he bought several suits—from $1.00 to $1.50 apiece—at auctions at the MGM studios. Although the jackets were occasionally tight across the middle and the pants' zippers strained, Hughes proudly showed the labels: "David O. Selznik" and "Spencer Tracy."

As Hughes slowly learned law in the courtroom, he became confident, especially in cross-examining prosecution witnesses about their drug habits. His big moment neared as the Thanksgiving holidays began. He would return to give final summation for his client, Leslie Van Houten. The consensus was that if any of the four Manson Family members were to walk away, it would be his client. There was little against her.

Hughes was planning to spend the weekend reading transcripts and putting together his notes in the wilderness. He was heading up to Ojai, California, about ninety miles north of the LA criminal courts building.

I liked Ron Hughes. He needed a ride that Friday evening, and I gave him a lift home. Ron lived in an old rundown house in a rundown part of town. He had rented the whole property, but he sublet the house in front and lived in the garage out back. He wanted me to read his closing argument, so I reluctantly walked back to the garage.

The inside was cluttered, not surprising, considering the number of hours we all spent at the courthouse. There were some paintings on the wall, and Ron told me he had done some of them himself. One he pointed out with pride was his diploma from law school. It was enormous, and he had colored it in so that it looked psychedelic. Pretty, but strange.

I looked for a clean place to sit down and read, while Ron—to my horror—starting relieving himself in a toilet that was to the side of the garage but not separated by walls or a door. It was just there, right there. I tried to read and not pay attention to him, but if there was ever a man of his times, it was Ron Hughes. A hippie in his heart, an artist, and a smart lawyer who wanted to save the world. A good guy.

His closing argument was excellent, and I told him so. He wasn't quite finished, but planned to complete it on his trip to Ojai. He didn't have a car—he hitchhiked to court every morning—but someone was going to give him a car for the weekend. While I was reading, he changed into old clothes, packed up his notes, and made ready for his trip. I had to go, and he walked me to my car and waved as I drove away. That was the last time I saw him. It was the last time anyone associated with the case saw him.

The following Monday, I went to the courthouse and heard the news that he was missing. At first I wasn't worried. Ron Hughes had been late to court three other times: once, he said he was delayed by rain; another time, he said his ride had failed to show up; the third time, he was in jail. So none of us worried, at least not at first.

On Monday afternoon, someone called the courthouse claiming to be Hughes. We never did find out who made that call. It was not Ron Hughes.

A rainstorm had hit the Ojai area that weekend. Mudslides and boulders came crashing down the hillsides, tearing out roads and turning dry streams into gushing rivers. Twenty-seven people were evacuated from the area, but Ron Hughes wasn't one of them. Searchers looked for him for weeks. Reporters, attorneys, and psychics joined the sheriff's deputies and forest rangers to hunt for any sign of Hughes or his body.

At first, prosecutor Vince Bugliosi claimed Hughes's disappearance was a hoax, then asked the judge to appoint a replacement immediately to avoid a mistrial. Bugliosi was never one to rest on sentiment. There was a short postponement of trial, but it went forward, no mistrial was declared.

If I had to guess, I think Charlie's girls killed him, and the storm just covered their tracks. The girls were feral. They would do anything for Charlie, even if Charlie didn't ask them to. Maybe they thought that if they killed Hughes, the trial would be postponed, and they could find a way to get Charlie out of jail. But there were two escaped convicts found in the area as well, and the sheriff's department speculated that maybe they had come across Hughes and killed him. No one knows.

Ron Hughes was a bit eccentric, but he had a good heart. He looked more like a hippie than a lawyer. Hughes talked to me because he knew that I believed he was doing a good job. To replace him, another attorney was appointed to take his place—conservative, straitlaced Maxwell Keith, a favorite of the judge with a commendable record as a defense attorney. He was liked by everyone—except his client, who immediately tried to fire him. It didn't work.

Irving Kanarek carried the ball for most of the trial, working hard for his client, even though Charlie objected almost daily to Kanarek's representation. Kanarek never gave up, objecting to testimony he saw as improper or prejudicial. He objected to Tex Watson being brought into the courtroom, saying Watson's appearance in front of the jury would be so damaging to Charlie's case that it would force a mistrial.

Kanarek questioned a witness named Danny DeCarlo, a member of a biker gang who had lived at the Spahn Ranch for a while, happily using the Family's women for sex, as Charlie had suggested. DeCarlo was an unpleasant character, almost repulsive.

Bugliosi wanted the court to recognize DeCarlo as a weapons expert because he claimed to be a gunsmith by trade. Kanarek objected. In an incident that would never happen in today's courtrooms, DeCarlo picked up the gun used in the Tate killings, pointed it at Kanarek, and pulled the trigger. The click of the trigger couldn't have been louder. Kanarek was clearly shaken. But he continued his cross-examination. You had to admire the guy.

In August 1970, Charlie and Judge Older had another in a long series of altercations.

"Your honor, this man is not doing what I want—not even by a small margin. He's not my attorney."

"I've reminded you not to speak out—" Here, Charlie interrupted.

"I would like to dismiss this man and get another attorney."

The judge turned to the jury and told them to ". . . disregard the statements made by Mr. Manson," and then he called a recess. They had barely filed out when Charlie started again:

> I've said to this court numerous times that I have no rapport with this attorney—no communication with attorneys, at least any that I have ever met. I've asked permission to question witnesses myself and operate behind other attorneys, but was denied.
>
> I took this man [Kanarek] as my attorney to file a motion before the federal courts to get my pro per back, but that's been delayed. Since then, I asked Mr. Kanarek not to do certain things and he does them. I've asked him to do other things and he won't do them. He does other things that are good, but I asked him not to ask certain questions but he asks them anyway.
>
> He's a sincere, honest, truthful human being and I like him very much as a person. But as an attorney he can't represent me—he doesn't represent me. In the eyes of the court I'm inadequate to represent myself, so I'm forced to remain silent—I've been told to do so on several occasions. But I can't bring him [Kanarek] to my thoughts. I have no control over his thoughts, and I can't express my words through this man.
>
> I would like to represent myself—it [the trial] would go so much faster and be less confusing. I would have very few questions to ask.

No one was surprised when Judge Older brushed off the request, for the umpteenth time, telling Charlie to find a way to get a "closer rapport" with his counsel, which Charlie said was "impossible."

It wasn't the first time Charlie had asked to fire Kanarek, and it certainly wasn't the last. At one point, the judge told Charlie he considered him "hopelessly incompetent" to defend himself, reminding him that four judges in four different courtrooms had made the same ruling. Charlie wouldn't let it go, arguing: "I'm asking for something which is at the very foundation of this country. I'm asking for a right my forefathers fought and died for." He added that Kanarek's questioning was like "trying to swat a fly with a baseball bat," and Charlie argued he would be a better advocate for himself.

It was at this point in the hearing that Charlie digressed. He addressed the "Helter Skelter" argument, Bugliosi's theory that the murders were an attempt to incite a race war: "We've heard a lot about helter skelter—everyone's saying what it's supposed to mean. Helter skelter only means confusion to me. If you look it up in the dictionary, that's what it will mean to you too."

Charlie desperately wanted to fire Kanarek. Charlie butted heads with him every day, and complained about him every week, but I thought Kanarek did his job well. He was fighting an uphill battle, against the judge and against his own client. In his summation, before the case was given to the jury, I think he hit the right note. He blamed everything on the prosecutor, Vince Bugliosi, saying Bugliosi had built his case against Charlie on insinuations, assumptions and possibilities: "We're supposed to be in this courtroom on matters that do not involve myths. This [the charges] is a figment of a particular prosecutor's imagination . . . a preconceived notion, thought about as a way to get Charles Manson. This is beyond belief. Mr. Manson is a human being with the same body temperature as everyone else. He has a normal this and a normal that. They've tried to substitute some kind of fantasy instead of proof. Turned him into some kind of deity. . . . or mystic."

Kanarek railed against the lack of evidence against Charlie, personally, and against Bugliosi's decision to try Charlie on the lifestyle of the Spahn Ranch Family members. Kanarek argued that the case "boils down to an unbelievable confrontation" between Manson's ideas and the establishment: "The criminal court is no place to carry on this type of confrontation. All of us in this courtroom have the power to end that confrontation by doing what the evidence in this case shows—that is to find Mr. Manson not guilty of all charges." Kanarek ended his argument just as he began by charging that Charlie was not on trial for seven murders, but was on trial because he was a symbol of what was wrong with American society.

It was a careful summation, but the jury wasn't impressed. Restless and fidgety throughout, they broke into smiles only when Kanarek said he was done.

Kanarek's shaggy long-haired client changed his look in the middle of the penalty phase. Charlie came into court one day dressed in a suit and dress shirt, with his head shaved, and his long beard trimmed into a neat goatee. But carved into his forehead was a Nazi swastika, still encrusted with blood.

In a written statement, he explained to the newsmen why he changed the cross he had etched into his forehead into a swastika: "I am what you are making me. I was good and now I know none. For you as a group of people have shown me no mercy. The mark on my head simulates the dead head black stamp of rejection; anti-church, falling cross, devil sign, death, terror, fear." Charlie provided an explanation for the swastika through his girls on the street corner. Again, how he got this information to the girls is a mystery. I don't think they would have made it up for him—they were too much in awe of their leader.

The day of the "new look," a writer was on the witness stand, talking about how a person—like Charlie—could easily manipulate someone who was on LSD. There had been a lot of testimony about how all the girls dropped acid routinely, and this witness claimed Charlie could easily talk someone high on LSD into murder.

After hours of listening to this, Charlie couldn't contain himself. He shouted, "There's two of us who knows he's ignorant—that's me and him. He don't know what he's talking about!"

Looking clean cut and wearing a suit hadn't changed anything. Judge Older told him to be quiet for the hundredth time, and Charlie sat next to Kanarek, fuming. When Kanarek gave his summation, arguing to keep Charlie out of the gas chamber, Charlie was not in the courtroom. The judge had kicked him out once again.

8 Prosecuting Charlie and His Girls

When this story began in August 1969, a wild-eyed nomad with the conservative, Midwest name of Charles Milles Manson was brought to the Inyo County courthouse in buckskins and in chains. He looked like a frightened caged animal, his eyes darting from newsman to newsman. More than a year later, after his conviction, he was no longer frightened. He had settled into what he told me was inevitable, even though it was obvious to me that he had hope of being acquitted, even on the day the jury filed back into the courtroom.

He was smiling the day the jury came back into the courtroom and smiling when the clerk nervously began to read the verdict. His smile soon faded, and he sat tugging at his beard. After the jury filed out, Charlie was brought to his feet and led out of the courtroom. He was heard muttering, "You'll never live to see that day." We thought it was directed at Judge Older, but what day and what he was referring to was—and still is—a mystery.

The first day of the trial, with the jury in the box, began July 19, 1970. I captured it for my readers:

> His long brown hair hangs to his shoulders—snarled and unkempt, hiding his face.
>
> His beard, at times clean cropped but more often growing uninhibited by a razor, shields a youthful face.
>
> Spectators and newsmen from throughout the world watch his every move.

Ohio tourists, in Los Angeles for only a day, forego Hollywood and Disneyland to sit in the courtroom and watch. A representative from the United Nations "drops by." County, city and state officials try to appear blase as they stop to catch what's going on.

They all come to see one thing.

Charles Manson.

By the time I wrote these words, I had developed a relationship with Charlie, and the difference between my early stories and the start of trial shows. I didn't ignore the obvious. I wrote: "He has been called the most demented, cold-blooded killer the world has ever produced." But I balanced that with a look at the man Charlie was or might have been: ". . . his eyes twinkle into a smile which is quick to come and quick to go. He winks, smiles, cocks his head to friends in the press and spectator section, but is stopped by two deputies sitting nearby if he attempts to stage whisper or mouth messages to them."

The prosecution's opening statement was presented by Vince Bugliosi. Bugliosi treated it as "show and tell" time, bringing his family and several television personalities with him. He jumped right into his "Helter Skelter" theory, telling the jury that "although evidence will show that Charles Manson hated black people, he also hated the white establishment, which he called 'pigs.'" Kanarek objected multiple times during the opening statement, even though objections during opening statements are not normally allowed. But Kanarek couldn't sit still while Bugliosi called his client "a vagrant wanderer, a frustrated pseudo-philosopher, but most of all, a killer who masqueraded behind the common image of a hippie, that of being peace-loving."

Charlie was smart—there was no doubt about that—and he demanded to conduct his own defense from early on, and he continued to complain that he should have a say in his defense for the next year, as the case moved from indictment to trial, and attorney after attorney was assigned to represent him.

Seven months before the start of trial, in December 1969, Charlie first asked to be his own attorney. In the story I wrote after that hearing, I called him a "hypnotic-eyed cultist." Less than a month later, he would agree to talk with me.

In that early hearing, Judge William Keene listened as four different attorneys wrangled to assist Charlie, who had told Judge Keene that he wanted to represent himself, with the aid of attorneys Luke McKissick and Lawrence Steinberg. The judge insisted Charlie accept a court-appointed attorney. Charlie pushed back but finally, worn down by the judge's insistence, accepted the judge's offer because he "couldn't refuse." Charlie told the judge that the media had already convicted, executed, and buried him.

One of the attorneys in the room, George Shibley, claimed to have been friends with Charlie since 1957. He then stood up and accused Judge Keene of forcing Charlie to take on a court-appointed attorney because the judge wanted to better his own chances of running for Los Angeles County district attorney. This brought a gasp from the onlookers.

When Charlie finally agreed to a court-appointed attorney, the four attorneys all spoke at once, asking to be appointed, but Judge Keene would not decide. He said he would make a decision after consultation with the bar association. I had never before heard of a judge consulting with local lawyers before making a decision. And the judge never revealed how that consultation went.

Of all of the participants in the case, Judge Charles Older—who ended up as the trial judge—was a mystery to me. He refused all interviews, not just from me but from the entire press corps. His reputation was as a straight-arrow, conservative, law-and-order man. He was appointed to the bench by Governor Ronald Reagan, just two years before the Manson trial. He was a World War Two veteran. But he was new on the job, and ended up with this complex, high-profile case, with four defendants. I was surprised he handled it as well as he did. But one of Older's friends and colleagues, state Supreme Court Justice Malcolm Lucas, said he was given the case because he was unflappable and unflinching, ". . . just like when he was a World War II Ace." Unflappable perhaps, but one member of the press corps later recalled, "He had absolutely no sense of humor. It was all business . . . It was a nutty trial. The only time we knew he was getting upset was when his cheeks would get red."

Judge Older did not have a reputation of being a "hanging judge," just a quiet man who did his job. As far as I was concerned, he didn't deserve that reputation. The day before the trial started, he took the unprecedented step of taking several pre-trial motions off calendar without a hearing, refused to hear several others, and told the attorneys that jury selection would begin Monday.

This followed on the heels of Charlie being carried screaming out of court by three bailiffs, while the three girls walked out, shouting at the judge the whole time. This was right after Charlie and the girls had pulled the crucifixion routine, holding out their arms and bowing their heads. We would get used to this, but at the time it was new.

A couple months later, clearly frustrated with Charlie's theatrics, the judge started taking testimony in his chambers. The defendants weren't there, and the press and public waited impatiently in the courtroom for news. This was a first in California jurisprudence. While hearing motions in chambers was relatively common—Judge Older had done that repeatedly—hearing witness testimony in chambers, without the defendants having a chance to hear the testimony, was brand new. Having covered trials for years, I couldn't understand how the judge could do this—but it was his courtroom, his rules.

Of course, Charlie objected loudly the first chance he got. The judge came back on the bench, and Charlie broke into song, signing a few bars of "That Old Black Magic," before being cut off: "That's what you're doing, judge . . . that old magic."

Judge Older said, "Let's continue," but Charlie wouldn't stop there: "May I suggest that the court continue to try itself. It's done a poor job of showing the public justice."

I think Judge Older did everything he could to make sure Charlie and the girls were convicted. He threw Charlie out of court multiple times, and the girls as well, all in front of the jury. He refused to let Charlie testify. Some of his rulings were clearly biased, and Charlie hated him.

By October 1970, Charlie and the girls were fed up. Judge Older came out from his chambers to take the bench, and Charlie and the three girls—Sadie, Patricia, and Leslie—jumped to their feet, gave the Nazi salute, and shouted, "Hail Caesar!"

Predictably, Judge Older told them all to sit down, but Charlie refused. The judge then told Charlie that if he didn't sit down, he would be taken out of court and returned to a holding cell. Charlie retorted, "I'd like to go back to my room.

I find it natural to do what I'm told." This led to a chaotic exchange, with Older shouting at Charlie to sit down and be quiet, and Charlie shouting at Older.

"You've charged me with murder and said I have rights but you don't give me my rights."

"Be quiet!" the judge shouted, "or I will have you removed."

"I'm not here anyway. You can put a picture up here and prosecute it."

Ignoring Charlie's complaints, the judge said, "We're going ahead."

Charlie interrupted again: "We're going ahead to where?" Then turning to the awed spectator section of the courtroom, he accused, "Look at all of you. You'll end up being judged. It's your judgment day, not mine."

Then Charlie turned and quietly left the courtroom. He really knew how to write the story for the press. This was good copy.

That same afternoon, the jury was about to be brought back into the courtroom, and Charlie started singing the song "The Old Grey Mare," but with new words:

The old grey mare she ain't what she used to be
She's now on the bench

"I admonish you to keep quiet!"

"But you're a woman, judge. You're acting just like a woman."

"I order you to stop talking—right now."

"You ordered me to stop living. You've deprived me of the right to counsel. I'm only allowed to talk to my attorney for five minutes a day while you're on the bench. You won't let me receive mail. You've limited my visitors to five minutes. How do you except me to get a fair trial like this?" Charlie was escorted from the courtroom again.

One afternoon, after all of the defense attorneys had passed on asking questions of a witness, Charlie politely asked, "May I ask a question?" The judge refused to answer him, so Charlie raised his voice: "Are you going to use this courtroom to kill me?" Still, Older ignored him. Charlie repeated the question: "Are you going to use this courtroom to kill me?"

Older kept ignoring him. Charlie warned, "If you are going to use this courtroom to kill me, you know what I'll have to do."

That got the judge's attention: "What will you do, Mr. Manson?"

Surprisingly, Charlie couldn't find the words, finally saying, "You know. You know." He went on: "You ordered me to be quiet while you kill me in this courtroom. I'm not going to just sit here and let you kill me. I'm a human being and I'm going to fight for my life—one way or another."

"I'll have you removed, Mr. Manson, if you don't be quiet."

Charlie shouted, "You think I'm kidding—"

Then, to the shock and surprise of everyone in the courtroom, Charlie lunged over the desk at the front of the courtroom, holding a pencil like a knife, and tried to reach Judge Older. Of course, two or three beefy bailiffs took down all 125 pounds of Charlie before anything happened. As he was dragged out, Charlie shouted, "In the name of Christian justice, someone should cut your head off!"

I later asked Charlie what the hell he was thinking: did he really think he could kill the judge? Charlie nodded. I asked, "With a pencil?" Charlie only laughed.

In hindsight, Judge Older may have been a product of the times. This was 1970, a year of terrible change and upset in the United States. The Manson jury was seated in June 1970. Only a few weeks earlier, the National Guard had killed four protesters and injured nine others at Kent State University. Protests against the Vietnam War were held in Los Angeles almost every week. Hippies, long-haired and barefooted, were a reminder that the "straight" people weren't in charge anymore. Bobby Kennedy was shot in June 1968 at the Ambassador Hotel, the same hotel where the Manson jury was being sequestered. The "silent majority" was being pitted against the "hippies," and "hippies" included anyone who protested the Vietnam War, anyone with long hair, anyone who wasn't in lockstep with the conservatives. The Nixon White House was telling the nation that the "hippies" were dangerous, communists, cowards.

In February 1970, an Army captain named Jeffrey MacDonald slaughtered his entire family, in a copycat killing to the Tate-LaBianca murders. He claimed "hippies" did it. By the time the Manson trial started, the public did not yet know that MacDonald was the real killer.

It is possible that Judge Older saw in Charlie Manson a face of evil, plastered on top of the "hippie" scare. I personally wrote that Charlie was a "hippie cult leader" in more than one story. That thought echoed around the country, and in newspapers around the world. Judge Older may have felt compelled to get a conviction and restore some semblance of order and sanity in a crazy and stressful time. I can't say for sure. But 1970 was a tough year for everyone.

I tried repeatedly to get Judge Older to give me an interview, but he would not. Whenever I would start on a case with a lot of public interest, I would do a series of stories focused on the participants: the judge, the prosecutors, and the defense attorneys. Except for Judge Older, I did that in the Manson case. Before the trial started, I did a story on Aaron Stovitz, a great guy and a seasoned prosecutor, and his younger second chair, Vince Bugliosi.

The story was about both prosecutors, and it read the way you would expect. I got some good quotes from Stovitz, and talked about Stovitz's reputation and his experience in the LA district attorney's office. Stovitz was the lead, the man selected by district attorney Evelle Younger to prosecute the most famous murder case in the world. Then I wrote about Bugliosi, as an up-and-coming prosecutor known for his successes. This was—to me—a "nothing" story, background only.

Unfortunately, I described Vince Bugliosi as "balding," and after that story he didn't say a word to me unless it included insults or vulgarities. He was furious. He came up to me after the story ran and said he had seen it and would make things difficult for me, in a diatribe full of words not fit to print. After that, Bugliosi would see me in the hallways of the courthouse and snarl a nasty word or a slur. He absolutely hated me, and I could not understand why. Was it the "balding" comment? Was that all it took to shake up one of the Los Angeles DA's best prosecutors? It would seem so.

Bugliosi's language was vile, and it was hard to get a good quote from him, because he peppered everything he said with things I couldn't print. What he said to me, personally, was much worse. He called me a name in the courtroom that I had never heard before, and I had covered the Los Angeles Waterfront for years. Bugliosi would hold press conferences during the trial, and after a while, the press wouldn't take it seriously. He was impossible to quote, rambling on in his high-pitched voice about how well things were going, even while all of us had been in the same courtroom as he was. And the press had seen him shout and swear at me and some of the other reporters. That didn't help his credibility.

Bugliosi even reported me to the district attorney himself, asking that I be taken off the case and barred from the courtroom. I met with the DA several times, and each time the conversation was more chewing the fat than discussing my failings or Bugliosi's. I don't know what was said to Bugliosi after those meetings, but I kept my front row seat at the trial, and Bugliosi kept swearing at me in the hallways.

Stovitz made some mistakes during the trial, violating the judge's gag order and some other things, but it was Bugliosi badmouthing Stovitz to the district attorney that led to Stovitz being removed from the case. Bugliosi was left in charge. Vince couldn't stand being second chair. His ego wouldn't allow it. There were a couple of young district attorneys assigned to the case to assist, but Bugliosi never let them say a word. One was Steve Kay, an exemplary prosecutor who eventually convicted Lawrence Bittaker and Roy Norris, two men who tortured multiple young women to death, recording the murders and playing the tapes back at orgies. Bittaker and Norris were nothing like Charlie Manson. I interviewed them as well, but never found any kindness in them, nor any humanity.

Bugliosi's ego couldn't share the spotlight with Stovitz, and when he got Stovitz bounced, it was his show. But the press couldn't stand him. We took a quick poll, and the press corps voted him the man they'd most like to see go to the gas chamber with Charlie.

Bugliosi's famous temper showed all through the trial. He claimed I was trying to turn the press against him, but he did that all by himself. In September 1970, perhaps halfway through the trial, Bugliosi got into a shouting match with Irving Kanarek, and it came to blows, with a prosecution witness being shoved into the jury box. Thankfully, the jury was out at the time.

Bugliosi's ire included the extended Manson Family. Outside the courtroom, one of Charlie's girls—Sandy Good—had been sitting outside the courthouse on the sidewalk, saying she would stay there until Charlie was released. She had kept her vigil for three days and nights before Bugliosi threatened her and called her obscene names. According to Kanarek, Bugliosi said, "I'm going to have you behind bars if it's the last thing I do. . . . and see that you get the death penalty." Bugliosi admitted that some of the things Kanarek told the judge were true, then hid behind the court's gag order and refused to answer any more questions.

Sandy Good never got the death penalty, although she did go to prison in 1975 for sending threatening letters to environmental polluters. She was the last one of Manson's inner circle to lose her freedom, post-trial. All the others, including several who had nothing to do with the Tate-LaBianca murders, were already in prison for everything from credit card fraud to murder. In one of the trial's stranger days, Good was put on the stand to testify that she had dated one of the prosecuting attorneys—Steve Kay—when they were both in high school. Kay squirmed in his seat as he listened to one of Manson's most loyal girls tell of the two of them going to a pancake house when she was fourteen and he was about a year older.

Late in the case, almost at the end, Bugliosi was talking to the jury about one of his witnesses, Barbara Hoyt, who once hitchhiked to Kansas City in search of her boyfriend. Sadie Atkins got to her feet and interrupted: "Ladies and Gentlemen of the Jury—Barbara Hoyt took LSD."

The bailiffs grabbed her to take her out of the courtroom, but Sadie grabbed at Bugliosi's notes as she was led past his desk by a bailiff, pushing the notes off his desk. He shouted, "You little bitch!" at Sadie's retreating back, in open court, in front of the judge and the jury. With his left hand, he grabbed at the notes, with his right hand, he took a swing at Sadie. Not exactly the actions of a seasoned professional prosecutor.

The huge headline over my story the next morning read "Manson Prosecutor Takes Swing at Susan." I had fun writing that story.

Sadie Atkins had testified extensively about the Tate murders, as well as the killings of Leno and Rosemary LaBianca. She spilled her story to the Grand

Jury in December 1969 and implicated Manson. She had been promised that the death penalty would be taken off the table for her testimony against the other defendants. But Bugliosi decided to back off of that deal.

I have a memo of a meeting from December 4, 1969, in which district attorney Evelle Younger and prosecutors Aaron Stovitz, Vince Bugliosi, and Paul Caruso were present, along with Sadie Atkins's then-attorney, Richard Caballero. It was decided at that meeting not to give Sadie immunity for her testimony, but it was agreed that Sadie's information was "vital" to law enforcement in solving the murders. As a result, the District Attorney agreed not to seek the death penalty. The agreement was literally in writing. And Bugliosi refused to honor that.

In his summation, Bugliosi spent a lot of time on his pet theories, including the race war and "Helter Skelter," theories all the defendants thought were ridiculous. But Vince Bugliosi couldn't help himself—he had as long as he wanted to sum up the evidence, and it was a free pass to say anything he liked. His temper and his ego took over. He made personal attacks on the defense attorneys, especially Irving Kanarek, which led to several motions for mistrial because Bugliosi's language was so inflammatory. He called Kanarek "deaf and blind" because he thought Manson should be acquitted. I had to roll my eyes—what did Bugliosi expect? For Manson's own lawyer to tell the jury he should be convicted? Bugliosi told the jury Manson sent the killers off to the Tate home: "It was your client, Mr. Kanarek, and he was waiting for them when they returned . . . The head zombie, Tex Watson, reported back to Manson, saying he told his victims, 'I am the devil, here to do the devil's work.' He also told Manson there was a lot of panic and it was messy with bodies all around but they were all dead. He was reporting back, 'Mission accomplished, sir.'"

Bugliosi told the jury that the scene was something "you don't even see in a foreign film": "Horrifying screams, rivers of blood that flowed from their bodies . . . the terror, horror, and savagery was unbelievable."

Relying heavily on the testimony of Linda Kasabian, who was the only witness who put Charlie at the scene of either murder, Bugliosi then talked about the LaBianca murders. Theatrically, nearly shouting, he turned to Kanarek and started berating him: "It was your client, Mr. Kanarek, who ordered these murders. It wasn't Genghis Khan or an aunt of mine who lived in Minnesota. . . . [The defense] simply didn't want to look at the evidence. It was poison to them."

Bugliosi said Kanarek was the "Toscanini of tedium . . . who has tied up this case for six months." Continuing with his opera references, Bugliosi added, "In every circus, there's a clown, and we all know who's playing Pagliacci here."

At this point, Charlie had been banned from the courtroom once again and was in a holding cell adjacent to the courtroom. When Bugliosi started criticizing Kanarek, Charlie growled loudly and shouted, "Are you trying Irving Kanarek? He's not my lawyer."

But Bugliosi wasn't done with Kanarek. He claimed that if Kanarek had said on television what he had said in the courtroom, he would be on trial for defamation of character. Bugliosi told the jury that if Kanarek's statements were true, "we should all pack our bags and leave the United States . . . we are no better than Hitler's Germany or Stalin's Russia. . . . There's no depth to which Irving Kanarek will not sink to get an acquittal."

When the defense lawyers objected, the judge instructed the jury to disregard Bugliosi's personal attacks on Kanarek. So he turned to Maxwell Keith, who had only been involved for a few weeks, having replaced Ron Hughes. Bugliosi called Keith a conservative lawyer from Pasadena, who "clouded the air so much that when he was through, Mayor Yorty should have called a smog alert."

Bugliosi acknowledged that there was very little fingerprint evidence. Only the prints of Tex Watson and Patricia Krenwinkel were found at the Tate house, and none of the defendants' fingerprints were found at the LaBiancas' house. Fingerprints from twenty-five other people were found, but none of them were Charlie's. I don't think he was there. He did his work through his Family. He told me more than once that he is a small man, a man who avoids physical fights. He wouldn't have been there when he had Tex Watson and Sadie Atkins to "do the devil's work."

The jury seemed to like the Helter Skelter theory, even asking to hear the Beatles' *White Album* during deliberations. Judge Older agreed with that request but turned down the request for the jury to visit the Tate and LaBianca homes after dark. I couldn't even imagine what they were thinking—how would seeing the houses at night help them find the Family innocent or guilty? Looking back, it would seem the jury was going stir-crazy, and thought a visit to the murder scenes would be illuminating. And it would get them out of the jury room for a change.

In 1971, during the penalty phase of the trial, Bugliosi asked the jury to hand Sadie Atkins the death penalty, despite the prior agreement not to. The district attorney's office pursued the death penalty against all of the defendants, not only Sadie. The defense called in then Attorney General Evelle Younger, because he was the district attorney when the deal was made. On the stand, Younger claimed his memory was "hazy," which I thought highly unlikely.

Younger was also questioned about the violation of the court's gag order. Shortly after Sadie Atkins testified to the Grand Jury, her confession to the murders was published by a newspaper (not mine). That was a clear violation of the court's ruling that the parties, the district attorney's office, and the defense attorneys would not speak of the case to the press, or anyone, for that matter.

Younger was also vague about how that story got in the papers. But that story—Sadie's confession—naming Charlie and the others was the catalyst for many of the stories that followed. The public was spoon-fed the cult angle, the LSD parties, the orgies. . . . all the things that made any potential jurors see Charlie Manson as the heart of evil.

Younger was running for higher office, and he liked the press coverage. I thought much of the controversy was part of Younger's strategy for more inches in print, more television time. And as for Bugliosi—well, he managed to make the trial last for ten months, and rode the spectacle for years, getting a book deal out of it and plenty of other opportunities.

Kanarek presented his final arguments on behalf of Charlie in January 1971. Charlie interrupted Kanarek at one point, shouting that he (Kanarek) "was only making it worse." After six days of argument, Charlie's patience ran out. Charlie typed up a formal motion and presented it to Judge Older. Again, Charlie insisted he had a right to represent himself, to present his own defense to the jury.

He wrote: "Mr. Manson himself wants to announce to the world and to this court how he has been misused for a stepping stone of the district attorney's office so they can let the world see what is their own thoughts and not of his or his co-defendants."

Charlie filed this brief at the end of the trial. For more than a year, he had been asking to represent himself, asking to be allowed to tell the jury that he was being railroaded, along with girls. He continued: "The defendants can produce witnesses who will rebuttal the language of the district attorney's office, the radio stations and all other comments of the press . . . It is the contention of the defendants that the lawyers . . . are simply using the Family Name of this case to claim publicity for themselves, not caring what happens to the defendants or their honored names."

Judge Older took Charlie's motion under submission, then the jury came back in. Within minutes, Irving Kanarek was continuing with his summation, telling the jury that if they found Charlie guilty, the state of California would be given a "license to shoot all hippies," claiming that "crowds in the street are calling for a guilty verdict." Kanarek seized on Vince Bugliosi's claim that the Tate-LaBianca killings were intended to incite a Black-white race war. Instead, he argued, a guilty verdict would "trigger a war against hippies which would give the state a license to shoot them all."

Bugliosi had argued Charlie wanted a race war, and Kanarek argued that the prosecution had drummed up a "fantastic" scenario, in order to get a guilty verdict "at any price." The charges against Charlie Manson were, according to Kanarek, "a figment of a particular prosecutor's imagination," built on "insinuations, assumptions and possibilities." Kanarek insisted that most of the prosecution witnesses were "mentally crippled" because all were "saturated with LSD."

Kanarek told the jury—which appeared bored through most of his marathon, eight-day summation—that Charlie wasn't on trial for seven murders, but for being a symbol of what is wrong with American society. There wasn't any evidence, he argued, to show Charlie was at the crime scene, that he ordered the murders, or that he conspired to commit the murders. In fact, Kanarek argued, the case boiled down to "an unbelievable confrontation between Manson's ideas and those of the establishment." Charlie should have loved this guy—he was saying what Charlie was telling me, only in different words.

Of course, Judge Older denied Charlie's motion to represent himself. Kanarek kept fighting, filing motions for a new trial, and working hard at the sentencing hearing, but it was a lost cause.

After the defense lawyers finished their closing arguments, Vince Bugliosi came back for his final argument. At times, he screamed at the jury and pounded the table. He called Charlie a "warped megalomaniac." He said Charlie had confessed to the murders when he threatened a witness by holding a knife to his throat. "We're dealing with a man," Bugliosi told the jury, "with a crazed, warped, twisted mind."

On the second day of his argument, Bugliosi was speaking when a nineteen-year-old blonde woman stood up and started shouting: "The prosecution has bribed, coerced and threatened key witnesses in this case, and I can prove it!" She was hustled from the courtroom by the bailiffs and kept away from the press. She later said she knew that twenty-five thousand dollars had been paid to one of the prosecution witnesses to get the right testimony before the court. I never did find out what she was talking about.

Bugliosi's anger, always just below the surface, showed clearly in this last hurrah of the trial. He accused one defense attorney, Paul Fitzgerald, of misstating the evidence, or at a bare minimum, of having failed to listen to the evidence during the trial. But he saved most of his ire for Kanarek.

This kind of personal attack on the other lawyers was highly unusual at the time. The fact that Judge Older didn't step into the fray until forced to do so says a lot about how the case was handled. Yet, despite this, after the jury left for deliberations, Judge Older fined Kanarek for interrupting Bugliosi's closing argument, but did nothing to Bugliosi for the continuing personal attacks against the defense lawyers.

Bugliosi got a little help during trial from then President Richard Nixon, who—in the middle of the trial—declared Charlie was guilty of the murders. Paul Fitzgerald tried to get a mistrial declared, calling Nixon's statement "unprecedented in American jurisprudence":

> I've got faith in the system that "truth, justice and liberty will prevail." That's how naive I am. But for a man who purports to stand for law and order to speculate and conjecture in regard to a person's guilt is unbelievable. . . . The President strikes me as a man who is in control of his faculties . . . it's hard to believe a man of public presence with the background of an attorney and statesman could be misunderstood. I wish he'd just leave us alone and let us try our lawsuit.

Despite his grandstanding, Fitzgerald didn't focus on how that information got to the jury—it was Charlie himself who held up the newspaper with the headline blaring, "Manson Guilty, Nixon Declares." Fitzgerald's motion for mistrial was denied.

Charlie did take the stand in his own defense, over Kanarek's objections. In fact, Kanarek had to be restrained by a bailiff as Manson walked to the witness stand, with Kanarek shouting the entire time. The jury never heard the twenty-seven minutes of testimony, but Charlie was at his best.

That day, I wrote that Charlie was "fighting back tears" as he testified, calling everyone "crazy": "If I could get angry at you, I would kill each one of you. If that's guilt I accept it. . . . I killed no one and I've ordered no one to be killed. I don't place myself as a secret judge." As I said, Charlie never stopped claiming he was innocent.

He continued, "You want me to be a sadistic fiend because that's what you are. But I don't care about any one of you. I'm not responsible for you. Your karma is not mine. You have to live with yourselves forever."

As for the Family's claims that he was the Messiah, Charlie said, "I may have implied to several people at several times that I was Jesus Christ, but I haven't decided yet who I am."

His anger bubbled over towards the end: "If I could fight you, I'd take this microphone and beat your brains out with it because you deserve it. You may destroy my body and tear my guts out, but you can't kill me. You can't kill a soul."

It might have been best that the jury didn't hear that. And honestly, I doubt Judge Older was listening.

Charlie finished his monologue and walked back toward his seat at the defense table. Judge Older asked the girls if they would like to make a statement. Sadie Atkins had just been handed a microphone, but as Charlie walked by, he said quietly, "Don't testify." Sadie—as always—obeyed. She handed back the microphone and told the judge she wouldn't testify.

Bugliosi's closing arguments lasted for several days, and his inability to curb his temper was front and center. Bugliosi compared Charlie and his love of animals to Hitler: "Adolph Hitler was very solicitous of his dog, Blondie, while writing the bloodiest chapters of world history. When Charlie Manson says he loves animals and thinking nothing of snuffing out of the lives of seven human beings, he's in good company."

It was during these last few days of trial that Charlie warned Bugliosi: "If I get the death penalty, there's going to be nothing but murder and bloodshed afterward, because I'm not going to take it." Bugliosi immediately turned around and told the press corps, in violation of the gag order.

That man loved the limelight.

Bugliosi spent his summation insulting the defendants, the defense attorneys, and many of the witnesses. On Bugliosi's final day of arguments, he turned to the jurors. Referring to the defense theories and their witnesses, he scolded the jury: "To believe their story, you would have to have the mind of a mentally retarded insect."

When the jury finally went out for deliberations, the county put the courthouse under what I called "martial law." It was the tightest security ever seen in the city. The jurors were escorted to a heavily guarded building in downtown Los Angeles by two sheriff's cars. The sheriff's official position was that this was "routine," but someone leaked a memo, saying that as soon as the jury began deliberations, the Hall of Justice was to be locked down, with security increased due to fears to "possible disruption."

Everyone coming to the courthouse was searched. All packages and containers were opened and inspected. Today, visitors to any county courthouse will find this routine, but in 1970 and 1971, the courthouses were wide open, no security, no metal detectors. I managed to get a copy of that confidential communique. It ordered that as soon as the jury began deliberation, the security for the Hall of Justice would "be increased due to intelligence reports of possible disruption." The presiding judge ordered that as soon as the jury started its work, there would be twenty-four-hour restricted access to the courthouse, which was to continue through the penalty phase. I never did find out what "possible disruptions" were expected or who reported them.

The jurors themselves were "crawling the walls," according to one report. Remember these jurors had been stuck with each other for almost seven months when they started deliberating, with only an occasional visit from family, and a rare outing, accompanied by sheriff's deputies. They lived in the Ambassador Hotel and were ferried to the downtown courthouse daily by the sheriff.

After a week of deliberations, the jury was in a circus mood, coming back from lunch one day carrying clown masks, which they used to decorate the sheriff's department bus that carried them to and from the Ambassador Hotel. As the bus, its windows clouded with scouring powder to prevent jurors from seeing street-corner newsstands, drove slowly past a crowd of reporters, one of the jurors smiled out through a giant peace symbol that he had etched in the Bon Ami.

Bugliosi was confident in the outcome. Before the jury even came back with a verdict, he had subpoenaed more than three dozen witnesses, persons who he expected to call in the penalty phase of the trial.

The day after buying the clown masks, the jury came back with a guilty verdict against Charlie and all the girls. Charlie listened to the verdicts being read, then shouted at Judge Older: "How come I've not been allowed to put on a defense? You won't outlive that, old man!" And without even looking at Charlie, Judge Older ordered him removed from the courtroom. Charlie had been repeating that mantra since the trial began, and he repeated it through the penalty phase, after sentencing, and while he was in prison. He believed the system had failed him completely.

No one was surprised by the verdict. In post-trial interviews with the jurors, one man told the press that "There was never any thought that they weren't guilty. . . . There wasn't anyone holding out for acquittal. And the death penalty was a clear cut thing. It was reached without too much trouble." Another juror, a woman, said she thought Manson was the clear leader of the group. She said, "I think he's a dangerous influence on society. In our verdict, we wanted to protect society." In hindsight, I think that sentiment should have been a red flag for the appellate court, but the verdicts were all upheld without any significant criticism of the judge or the lawyers.

On the first day of the penalty phase of the trial, Charlie rose quietly, again asking to be his own attorney and again being denied that right. Charlie said the trial had gone on for eight months, that he had no more money to pay his attorney, and that he had information that could help substantially in the penalty phase.

Judge Older shrugged it off and denied the request, saying the question of self-representation had been considered a half-dozen times, and he saw no reason to reason to change his mind.

"No man can speak for this man standing in front of you," Charlie told the judge. "These attorneys wouldn't understand a defense if it was put in front of them." Judge Older told him to sit down, but he refused.

"We wanted to put on a defense . . . I wanted to put on a defense from the time I was arrested," Charlie said. "The sheriff has more power than you have. You say something. The sheriff does another. Your orders don't flow." He added, "I ask to be allowed to put on a defense in this penalty phase . . . as clumsy and inadequate as it may be, you'll see a defense."

Judge Older again told Charlie he was ruling against him, but Charlie interrupted the judge and continued, raising his voice: "There's no way I can think through this man," gesturing at Kanarek. "There's no way I can speak through any of these people. There's no way I can express myself, even from the witness stand. You don't believe me because I say it. I want to call witnesses. What good is a courtroom if it's one-sided?"

Judge Older cut him off, telling him to "stop arguing" and sit down.

At this point, Charlie was shouting: "It's not an argument, it's a fact!"

"Sit down, Mr. Manson!" The judge shouted back.

"I'm supposed to sit here like a dummy. . . . there's no justice here, Older."

Judge Older told Charlie that if he kept it up, he would be removed from the courtroom, and "it would be in your best interests if you remained."

Charlie sank into his chair, mimicking the judge with a big sigh, saying, "My best interests. My goodness. My best interests. You've already convicted me of something that I haven't done. If you let me go in there [indicating serving as his own attorney] I'd tear that little boy apart . . . and you know it too." That last line about the "little boy" was directed at Vince Bugliosi.

At this point in the proceedings, Kanarek interrupted both Charlie and the judge with a complete non-sequitur. He stood up and claimed that one of the jurors had "taken to alcohol" during the sequestration. Judge Older turned to Kanarek and told the attorney to file a formal motion.

Shortly after that, with the jury in the courtroom, Charlie slugged Kanarek on the shoulder a couple of times, muttering "I can't communicate with you." When Kanarek objected to certain testimony, Charlie yelled at him, saying, "Would you be quiet, man! You're cutting my throat! Sit down!" The bailiffs stepped in and Charlie was ordered out of the courtroom again.

The constant battles between Charlie and Judge Older, and Charlie and Irving Kanarek, were only part of what Charlie was dealing with. In the early days of his confinement, his jailers hit him with all sorts of rules that didn't seem to apply to any of the other prisoners, and that had continued, more or less, though the trial. In November 1970, Charlie filed a complaint with Judge Older that he had been told he couldn't sing in jail.

Charlie's complaint contended that since he had been arrested in late 1969, he had been able to sing "in reasonably modulated tones" during the early evening hours. He said that as a "composer and performer," singing gave him "pleasure, enjoyment and reward . . . and allows me to express myself and relax. . . . I in no way interfered with the orderly administration of Los Angeles County jail . . . or the tranquility in the jail. My singing was not loud, boisterous and-or disruptive in any fashion."

Nevertheless, his jailers ordered him to stop singing. Clearly a distraction, Charlie was facing a more serious problem. Kasabian came back to testify, as did many other prosecution witnesses, all reiterating why Charlie and the girls should be sent to California's gas chamber at San Quentin.

In the middle of the penalty phase, after eight months of sequestration, Judge Older shocked the courtroom by announcing the jury could finally go home.

The judge warned the jury not to talk to anyone about the case but allowed them to return to their homes and families. He strongly warned the press not to talk with the jurors or attempt to contact them.

Although we can't be sure, the press assumed the release of the jurors was the result of a phone request by one of the jurors. Larry Sheely, a maintenance man from Paramount, said he couldn't stay any longer. He said his wife was unable to cope with the fact that he was away from home for so long, so the judge excused him from the panel.

The name of an alternate juror was chosen, a housewife from the San Fernando Valley. She asked to speak to the judge in chambers, and he refused. She was sworn in, but before she could take her seat in the jury box, she fainted. The next day, she went to the hospital due to a possible heart attack. The judge then seated another alternate.

Just another crazy day at the Manson trial.

A few days before this happened, Charlie issued a press release from jail, calling all the lawyers in the case "educated morons and intellectual midgets." The press release, which the press, jaded by months of the circus, mostly ignored, continued with an apocalyptic flare:

"I am not the King of the Jews nor am I a hippie cult leader."

I have to believe that was a little slap at my stories.

"I sit in your torture chamber. You have showed me no mercy, compassion or pity. And in my mind's eye my thoughts light fires in your cities. Here's what you are hiding from yourselves. Your days are in number and you're afraid to look. Go to the children and ask for forgiveness as your days turn to night."

I asked Charlie about Kanarek, but I didn't get much. Charlie wanted the opportunity to speak directly to the jury. He believed that he could get through to them, even while Kanarek couldn't. Kanarek was making objections to testimony as irrelevant and hearsay, and he was probably right . . . at least part of the time. But the judge kept ruling against him, and Charlie seemed to think that Kanarek's objections were harmful.

In October 1975, during an exchange of letters with Charlie, I told him that I agreed—he should have been able to act as his own attorney and put on the defense he wanted. I wrote to him:

> I think if anything overturns your case, it will be that point. The judge, in my book, was in error by not allowing you to defend yourself. Even Joe Ball (whose probably one of the most respected lawyers in the country) pointed out that you had the know-how to do it. If they felt you needed help on the legal technicalities, they should have assigned you a public defender or attorney to help you out on the briefs, etc. I haven't seen any of your latest appeal briefs, but I would think that would be all laid out in them. They're allowing Squeaky [Fromme] to do that now—where was that judge when you were asking the same thing? I know you're probably interested in that case. . . . so let me know if you are getting newspaper clips of what's going on . . . if not I'll send some along.

All of the appeals failed, errors or not.

The penalty phase saw multiple witnesses testifying about other crimes Charlie committed, including the shooting of a musician after a drug deal went wrong, and the Gary Hinman and Shorty Shea killings.

During the penalty phase, just a few days before all four of the defendants were sentenced to die in the gas chamber, Charlie issued a statement through his followers, the girls holding vigil outside the courthouse. It was classic "I am you and you are me" Charlie:

"I wanted to be a good guy but you didn't let me. I make a motion that Nixon gave me this country . . . it is either a state of total anarchy or total control. A brand new Young America with no weakness. A brand new world with love and peace. When I die, I don't die, the world dies. I have always lived and I will always love. . . . Much is coming. Much needs to be done."

My first reaction was that this was just more of Charlie's rambles. In retrospect, it was his farewell, expecting to be sentenced to death, expecting to be executed.

But he didn't die. The death sentence was commuted to life in prison. And Charlie had a lot more to say.

9 Charlie in His Own Words

Talking about his alibi for the Tate murders, Charlie said, "I pride myself on truth—even when it hurts."

When we talked about his life and the murders, Charlie always told me he was telling the truth. I didn't believe him, but he gave a great interview.

In one of our earliest conversations, Charlie opened up about his early family life. "To tell the truth," he told me, "I've never had a mother. I've been to prisons—one kind or another—from the time I was nine until I was nineteen. The last time I heard from my mother was when I was nineteen and ready to get out of prison. She wrote to me and told me to come home now and take care of her. She hadn't 'taken care' of me from the day I was born."

Charlie went home anyway. He didn't have anywhere else to go. Many years later, after his conviction, Charlie told me he never knew love after the age of ten. That made me very sad. No one deserves that.

He did love his grandmother, telling me she was a Kentucky Puritan and the only person who ever told him the truth: "She had the spirit of truth. She never read anything except the Bible, never left the house to go to a movie or dancing or anything. Never even cut her hair. She just read the Bible and filled all her kids with so much religion they regurgitated it."

His mother ran off when she was young, and the rest of the family ended up in prison too. "All of them," Charlie told me, "ended up bad, but that goes way back. Her grandpa cut off somebody's head, and her daddy did something else. It was in the family."

> When I was in prison, I thought all the good guys were on the outside and all the bad guys inside. I thought, "Man, I want to get out to join the good guys." But when I got out, a guy asked to borrow $20 until Friday. He never paid me back. The guys in prison always paid me back. And you know, people on the outside have lied to me all my life—just like the guy that borrowed the $20. They started by lying about Santa Claus. They lied about Superman—I thought I could fly for a long time.
>
> And they made me lie. I had to lie when I got our of prison. I had to lie to get a job, lie to people about my past so they'd like me, lie to get girls.

He told me that after getting out of prison in 1967, he finally faced the world with no illusions, no lies, and no dreams: "I had a real ego collapse. I finally realized I wasn't big and strong and handsome. I finally realized I was just me. . . . The things that happen to you in the past—your mother and father and their teachings—are what you are. Unless," he said, stroking his beard, "you can break through." And that is what Charlie said he had done. "My background is rotten, but a diamond develops under pressure. A Negro is more aware than a white because of pressure." He paused then, silent, searching my face, waiting for his words to penetrate: "I hate people being used—and that's what wives and mothers do." That might explain why Charlie created his own Family, with him securely in charge, calling all the shots: "Girls will follow if you love them enough. . . . think about them and not yourself . . . On the Ranch I tried to show that love is all there is. We'd sit around and I'd try to get them to forget all of the 'don'ts' their mother and fathers taught them."

He said he was one of society's "garbage people." He explained this one day, late in the trial, to Judge Older: "Where does your garbage go? We have tin cans and garbage along the side of the road, and oil slicks in the water—so you have people, and I am one of your garbage people. I'm one of those little scrawny nobodies that eats out of a garbage can, that nobody wants, that has been dragged through every hell hole you can think of. You expect to break me? Impossible. You broke me years ago. You killed me years ago."

Charlie described how his Family came together and he told me—I think he truly believed—that his girls, his Family, were his to protect. This wasn't an act.

> These children that come at you with knives—they are your children. You taught them. I didn't teach them. I just tried to help them stand up. Most of the people at the Ranch that you call "the family" were just people that you did not want, people that were alongside the road, that their parents had kicked them out or they didn't want to go to juvenile hall. So I did the best I could and them up on my garbage dump and I told them this: that in love there is no wrong.
>
> I have one law I live by and I learned it when I was a kid in reform school. It's "Don't snitch," and I have never snitched and I told them that anything they do for their brothers and sisters is good, if they do it with a good thought.
>
> It is not my responsibility. It is your responsibility. It is the responsibility you have towards your own children that you are neglecting, and then you want to put the blame on me again.
>
> You make your children what they are. I am just a reflection of every one of you. You only give them your frustration, you only give them your anger, you only give them the bad part of you rather than give the good part of you. You should all turn around and face your children and start following them and listening to them.
>
> I said let the children loose and follow them. That is what I did in the desert. That is what I was doing, following your children. . . . the ones you didn't want, each and every one of them. I never asked them to come with me. They asked me.

Always, Charlie insisted he did not commit the Tate-LaBianca killings, and he didn't ask his Family to commit the murders. In jail, in March 1970, he told me, "I know what I've done and what I haven't done. My conscience is clear. They have no case against me . . . and making a case against me is like trying to carry sand in a sieve. It can't be done." He never wavered from that. He repeatedly said he was protecting his family: "I showed them the best I could. What I would do as a father to a human being, responsible for themselves, but to be weak is not to lean on. I have told them many times. . . . I don't want weak people around me. If you're not strong enough to stand on your own, don't come and ask me what to do." Charlie made this speech in court in June 1970. My notes don't tell me the reason for the speech. As I have said, every day in the courthouse was another day in a three-ring circus, so it could have been prompted by any number of things. As of the date of the transcript, June 1970, the jury had yet to be sworn in, so this was for the benefit of the court and—of course—the press. In looking through my notes from that time, I found excerpts that I had culled from transcripts of hearings and the trial. Charlie had been silenced over and over, but sometimes the judge let him talk. When he couldn't talk in court, he talked to me. He had a need to get his story out to the wider world.

Charlie said he never murdered anyone, and that he didn't force his girls—or any of his family—into drug use. He said it was just the opposite: "They say I've strung people out on dope. I say to the kids—'Why take dope—just leave home—you don't need dope.'" Charlie said there was good dope and bad dope. Good dope, it was explained to me, expands the mind, makes you more aware. Bad dope just screws you up. At the Ranch, Charlie approved of LSD and marijuana or hashish, but did not approve of speed or heroin. Charlie told me that he got the teenaged daughter of a Hollywood actress off the "bad dope," only to find out that she went back on the drugs when her mother came back to California from New York. The star's name was one of the things mentioned off the record during our many meetings. Charlie said of the daughter: "I got her off speed . . . that's bad stuff. She was fourteen and had tracks up her arms like you'd never believe. But her parents came back home and now she's on heroin." She was just a kid, Charlie told me, and he loved kids.

Charlie often spoke about his family as children, that he was protecting them from the world, from their parents, from society. While he spoke of love, his anger often boiled to the surface. The court transcript continued like this: "If I could get angry at you I would try to kill every one of you. If that's guilt, I accept it." When he had the chance to get on the stand—never in front of the jury—he spoke of violence. I don't think he could help himself, he was so frustrated with the situation.

Before the Spahn Ranch, before the Family, most of Charlie's life was spent in institutions. Reform school, jail, prison . . . that was Charlie's life. In June

1970, Charlie was thirty-five years old, only five-foot-three on a good day, and 125 pounds. He told the judge:

> I survived twenty-three years in every torture chamber you have in this country, and I survived by bringing the good out in each human being. You can call it fear. I am afraid. I am a coward and I am brave. I am neither one.
>
> I have done the best I know how and I have given all I can give and I haven't any guilt about anything because I have never been able to see any wrong. I looked at it wrong and it is all relative. Wrong is if you haven't got any money . . . wrong is if your car payments are overdue. Wrong is if the TV breaks down. Wrong is if President Kennedy gets killed.

In our private conversations, when Charlie told me about his early life, he spoke of his mother. She was in and out of jail, a hard drinking woman. By thirteen, he was in what he called a reform school. There is no question that the school was harsh, beating the boys for the smallest infraction of the rules. Charlie said he would escape and sleep in the woods. Because of his size, he was always on the defensive. There are stories he was raped in reform school, but he never told me that.

With the exception of his Kentucky grandmother, whom he loved, Charlie didn't have anything nice to say about anyone, other than his girls and his Family. He told me his life had been very hard, and often violent. He said he wanted peace—and he found that in the desert with his Family:

> My peace is in the desert or in the jail cell and had I not seen the sunshine in the desert, I would be satisfied with the jail cell, much more over your society, much more over your reality and much more over your confusion, and much more over your world and your word games that you play.
>
> All I want is to be just at peace—whatever that is. Now in death you find peace, and soon I may start looking in death to find my peace. I have reflected in your society yourselves, right back at yourselves, and each one of these young girls is without a home.

But he knew he was never going to make it back to the desert sunshine. Talking to me, his optimism would waver, and he would tell me that he had already been "crucified" or that he was being battered by the system and would be executed. He knew.

Yet he tried to convince me that he was rallying, that he would present a defense and be out of jail and back to the desert before long. This is from an interview I did with him in jail in March 1970:

> "I'm a dead man speaking from the grave, but pretty soon I'm going to rise up and instead of just waiting for this thing (the prosecution case) to fall apart, I'm going to take the offensive. That's funny, isn't it? The dead man taking the offensive—him but I'm going to do that, and when I rise up, I'm going to bring as many minds with me as are willing to look at and accept the truth. I believe there will be a lot of them."

Charlie was right. A lot of people did believe him. Charlie received hundreds of letters in jail and he showed me a few. A typical letter was one from a ninety-year old ex-schoolteacher from Iowa, who had read of his "plight" in her local newspaper and had particularly disturbed by a picture of Charlie taken at the age of fourteen in Indianapolis. She offered help. Charlie wrote her a three-page letter, adding a postscript: "Please don't grade my spelling."

Many of the letters were about finding Jesus and urging Charlie to pray. One from a boy in Fresno, California, asked Charlie, "What magic do you use to get those girls?"

The guards apparently had the same question. Charlie told me that the guards in the jail had him strip, more than once. They would look at him standing naked, and talk to each other, asking how Charlie—small and skinny—could be so attractive to women, able to put together a family of girls, all of them willing participants in the sex play that went on at the Ranch. This type of humiliation continued when he went to one prison and then the next. Targeting the small man with the oversized reputation was apparently a popular game.

But prison was yet to come. In 1970, Charlie was in LA County Jail and received hundreds of letters from the public. Charlie was tickled by the delivery of some of the letters. He called it "phenomenal": "It's just plain out of sight how all those letters reach me. Get a load of this—it's from Iowa and just addressed to 'Charles Manson, Los Angeles, California." Other writers had read about Charlie's often-lengthy musings on love. One man from Sacramento, California, wrote that he had "reached understanding" through Charlie's words about love. Charlie spoke often about love: love for his family, love for animals, love that he said would change society.

On the flip side of that, there were multiple stories of Charlie physically abusing Family members. One woman testified at trial that she had followed Charlie to Spahn Ranch, and then out to Barker Ranch in Death Valley. But she wanted to go home. Charlie asked her if she was homesick. She said she was and wanted to go home. She then told the jury, with a weak smile on her face, that Charlie picked up a rifle and hit her across the head with it a couple of times, telling her that she better forget about going home.

The reverential statement of another girl couldn't help but echo: "He loves us so much, you just can't help but love him back."

This was the difficulty of dealing with Charlie Manson. He was a contradiction, a dark and violent man one minute, a loving and sweet leader of his Family the next.

Over the years of knowing Charlie, he must have sent me dozens of letters. But I only found a handful that I saved. I just didn't think that my correspondence with him would be interesting to anyone except me, especially because we had an agreement that what he said to me was just between us—unless he agreed to it. But Charlie died a few years ago so I think our deal is off.

We hadn't talked for some years. I was getting old myself, but I had read that Charlie wasn't doing well and was in the prison hospital. I wrote to him, asking if I could come see him just one more time. I followed up with a phone call, but he was in the hospital ward, and I couldn't reach him. The nurse promised to ask Charlie if I could come, and I was supposed to call back the next day.

I did. He said to come. He was near Bakersfield, in the middle of California, and I was in Los Angeles to the south, but I arranged for a ride. Before I could make it, his death from heart failure was announced.

I was surprised by my reaction, although I shouldn't have been. I was sad, regretting that I had waited too long to see him. He was one of the biggest stories I had ever covered. I was nominated for the Pulitzer Prize twice—and the stories with Charlie were the basis for the first of those nominations. And I liked him. I know it doesn't make much sense, but I liked him. He was smart, funny, interesting. And he may have been a killer—at the very least, he was responsible for the death of Shorty Shea or Gary Hinman. He certainly did nothing to stop the Tate-LaBianca killings, although he was almost certainly not at either of those crime scenes.

Charlie's letters are in his voice, with his misspellings, his grammatical mistakes, and his clear intelligent voice. As I said, I don't have many of them left; some of Charlie's letters to me are on exhibit at the Alcatraz East Crime Museum in Pigeon Forge, Tennessee. But here are some of the things he wrote to me in 1975, well after trial had finished, as he was settling in to what would be forty-two more years in prison.

As background, I left the country for almost a year, beginning in 1975, working with a newspaper in Central America, helping to shape an American-style journalism style to help democracy grow, so when Charlie mentions that I am leaving, that is what he is referencing.

This first letter is from March 1975:

> *Mary*
>
> *Did you git the letter I sent you right about the same time you left—??*
>
> *Go to Llema Peru—I've got a good frind there—His uncle ran for office in the government.*
>
> *Any way I got your card + thanks—I still never got the interview with anyone—the games being played around me reminds me of the dogs running after a girl dog + none wanting the other to get attention + each other trying to prove themselves—Everyone wants to fight for what I'm trying to git out of doing—Anyway anyway you be good to you + I'm there in that if you love you I do* [here, he drew a happy face]

This was pretty typical of Charlie. He would write about his contacts with the press, compliment me, complain about prison. But then he would go into detail about how he was railroaded, and how the system was stacked against him:

I feel it is not up to me to make the law obay the law—Joe Ball said the LAW said I can put my case in a court of law + if I can't then there is no court of law It's a phoney face for the money $ + power sick people who are turning the US in the hole—yes I put you where you put yourself—I had no frinds so I got none—you all git your own reflections + your own judgments.

Your a joke on your selves—you won't fix your courts as I right so you want the Death penalty + your kids see that's what your all working for + the 13 year old that did his mon + dad + sister gave what you are far so don't blame your children for doing just what your asking for—I tryed with all I had to wake you but I'm made in to the worst for it. You all want + keep me down + I don't see how your gona git under it—I've come up befor on earth + you wouldnt let me put on a defense or talk in your courts so history circles and repeats its self—you say you hurt—29 years in a cage and the last 7 years in solitary confinement leaves me thinking about your little hurts if you miss your change for a part.

*Tryl—all you denied me you will be denied—*No Mercy *is what you all have worked for in my eyes + don't say you're a friend of mine—you could of sent me a lot of pictures but only when you thought of an interview or wanted to get some ____ information—you a snake + I should of seen you the first time I seen you + loved your gentleness—I thought you had grase + class but your just a dirt digger—Keep my letters to you for they are to you only. I'd like to git you by your self alone in a room where no one could know I had you + I give you 1000 interviews—Green (LuLu) can't ask me to answer what shes saying + shes only saying what you all want to here—she don't know but a little bit of the thoughts set in you brains—Shes doing what she doing for her self + thats OK. She knows I never told her to do anything.*

Shortly after this letter, two men attacked Charlie in the prison yard at Folsom. The associate warden said Charlie was using the exercise yard there for the only the third time in the two and a half years since he had been transferred to Folsom from San Quentin's death row. "He's a recluse," said the warden. "He doesn't associate with people and he doesn't say anything to the staff. He just sits quietly in his cell most of the time, just sits and stares."

One of the men who attacked Charlie in the prison yard was Kenneth Como. The strange part about this is that Como was convicted in 1973 in a robbery that was part of a plan to free Charlie from prison. At his sanity hearing, Como testified that he was willing to fight and die for the Manson Family: "All I wanted to do was live, fight and die for those people. That was my attitude then and that is my attitude now." Like Charlie, Como had spent about half his life in prison or juvenile facilities. Yet only two years after saying he would fight and die for the Family, he tried to kill Charlie. From what I know of Charlie, the betrayal would have stung more than the beating he received. To add salt to the wound, a year after the attack on Charlie, Gypsy Share—one of the girls who showed me around the Spahn Ranch during the trial—married Como at Folsom Prison. By 1976, Gypsy was under federal indictment for a complex credit card scam.

The next letter I have from Charlie is dated September 1975. I had not been writing to him, because I had been out of the country. His loneliness was growing. He had spent a few years with his Family, but now he had no one. He was a small man, the guards had it out for him, and he was a famous killer. Prison life had to be tough for him.

> *Mary—This is between* me + you *+ not press*
>
> *I was just thinking about you. How's that hot body? Its so dam hard to stay on the safe side of everyone now days. Dam spot you* all *put me in has been a ruff one—ruff is like mean. But that's not me—it's a shame you all wouldnt lissen to me—but who would of understood—im so simple that a complicated mind only sees its own complication an visa versa.*
>
> *I don't remember any windows in the County jail—as I would of seen a door on the floor.* [he inserted a happy face here] *Did I miss something—I don't do that often you* all *let the DA git away with braking the laws + blameing me. If you reverst the hole thing, you would have more like the truth. If he wins the case + it keeps on going on in the minds of all them people He will get his Helter Skelter—I played the cards as they came to me + done as best to reflect it. Happy landings. Had I been aloud to put on a defence I could of put it right as it is its not got any better since I was in LA—if the DA keeps proving his case it should be a mud fate* [smiley face] *as a nut house. Everyone got there chance to judge me + I got no voice + no one wanted to*

here [hear] *it—I'll see anyone who I can—I wont go all hand cuffed _ leg irons but if you can come with the rest Im the same as I was the first day you slipped into see me–*

Neiswender is a good name for you +you were one of the best of the worst. [he inserted a happy face here] *Ide like to ask you a favor + if you do me this favor Ill make sure you git what you ask me for—Send me some photos from* <u>*all*</u> *the people who were in the so called Family—Im getting up a photo album but something to do + would like to git some (a lot) of photos of everyone + one of you to—your one of the few that put some good in your paper for us—Go to your photo lab + pick some of the hole trup for me—and remember you were the only reporter I ever really talked to from the press + that should of done you some good. So reflect some of that back. Don't send things all at once. A few at a time—So do that for ne—If there is any more needed for copys Ill send it to you–*

Remember there was 30 some people I got busted with. I would like one from all that I can git + you got an inside track to give me some of the good ones they hid—take a day for me + do that little job + one day I may be able to do you a favor—I may know some more things that would give you a rysan [reason?] *things no one els even thought of yet.* [he inserted a happy face here] *I sure would like some pictures of Boby Beausoleil, Charles Watson, Leslie Patricia Mary Brunner Gypsy Caysey Susan Steve Grogan + Dany Retclas + all the people you all said was a family.*

At this point, he was trying to get me to take the time to send photos, which I did in my reply. He closed with a reference to our favorite prosecutor:

Who know you may run Bugliosi out of town + be the one to sue him I could sue everyone but im too lazy—anyway you do that for me Mary. Behold your servant

I wrote back, saying:

First of all, when you ask a small favor you don't have to promise me anything in return. We had a good thing going between us when we had our talks—I think it was honest. I'd be glad to get some pictures up to

> you. Am sending a couple now and some each time as you suggested. Let me know if you receive them. However, I don't want you to promise anything in return—I wouldn't do it if I didn't want to no matter what the promise. If I worked that way I probably would have been on the side of Bugliosi.

In 1975, someone interviewed Sandy Good, who had been outside the courthouse with the other girls for the entire trial. At the time of the interview, Squeaky Fromme had just been arrested for trying to assassinate then President Gerald Ford. Gypsy Share was in jail for credit card fraud. Sadie Atkins had recently given an interview from prison, claiming that she was no longer part of the Family.

But Sandy Good said the Family was still together, spiritually. "Manson," she said, "is in a way the head of it [the Family]. In what way? I can't say, 'cause I don't know. He can send thoughts [from prison] in many, many ways that go beyond our rational understanding."

Charlie was definitely a spiritual man, but it was a religion of his own making. When he went into his "I am you and you are me" routine, it was hard for me to sit still. Sandi Gibbons, who covered the trial with me as one of the "sob sisters" in the front row, remembers Charlie's "I am you, you are me" speech as a way Charlie used to ensnare his followers. Everyone and everything was "one." When it was two, a second person, it was simply the "one" broken in half. But Charlie's routine on oneness wasn't a spin on Eastern philosophy. Instead, Charlie was the "one," the center of everything, and anyone else was just a part of him, a fraction of him.

This is from a transcript of a talk I had with him after his conviction. It is undated, but it is post-conviction:

> Are you here? If you are where you are, then you are the center of the world to you. The world was given to you when you were born. Teachers will try and teach of the past history, but nonetheless the world didn't exist before you. When you see you, you will also see you are one with everything. Once you're here, meaning strong within yourself, then you're in my heart and our hearts are a small part of God's heart. You

> can never go back or retrace steps taken. Everything being perfect, there is no backwards, only forwards, or one could say forwards-backwards. There is always change but progress only exists in man's mind.

He went on like this for a while. I think this is how he spoke to men and women, his Family, and they would join with him and would do whatever he asked. I'm afraid I couldn't see the attraction. He was persuasive, but the "I am you, you are me" patter didn't hold me, as it did so many others.

The transcript shows that Charlie went on for a long time in this vein, speaking of love, peace, the oppression of the church, and the "man":

> Me, I, we, or them, as you are not important to anything but yourself. The power gave you will, that will must be given back in order to reach or become on with your god—whoever he is to you. We see in our world that soon if we don't give up to his love he will take it anyway. Soon we will not have a choice, for karma is turning faster and faster.
>
> The Bible tells us that, if you can see past the words and see past the preacher who runs people away from the word of God that he makes so holy.
>
> When one takes a pencil in his hand and starts putting words on paper, he and word fall further from now. Never did JC [Jesus Christ] or anyone who was in tune with God write down anything. For when you reach this state of awareness you will see what a joke it all is. Everyone, through the illusion of time, tells us all this, but never do they tell you how to reach for peace.
>
> Mainly, none of them know anything except what's been read in a book. Over a hundred thousand people died on crosses to show with action how it's to be done in the last days. All the church has tried to do is hide this fact by putting JC out in front. JC was not out in front, for in love there is no leader, no followers. In love you are one together, none in front or behind. When one reaches this one in love, he is the other, coming together forming a new world.

Later in this conversation, he turned to his pending appeal:

> This court is going to try and pass judgment on me again, and once again as I have always been by myself and with others who are standing strong in their love by themselves . . . they will know us as we know them. Many times we have been in one court or another. We know we only see outside ourselves, what's inside ourselves, assured and what the world will make of us. All the things they think of themselves . . . so in reality, they will judge themselves as they are doing in the papers, magazines and on television. HA!
>
> We do not judge people, they judge themselves. We love the world, and if it doesn't love us, we do not care. We live with our love and it grows with every breath.

At this point in time, Charlie was aware of the accusations that the Family was committing crimes all over the West, and he was certain that his Family, his girls, his followers, were not involved. That's not what I heard.

I wrote a story in October 1979, based on my sources in local and federal law enforcement. They had strong evidence that some of the Family were banding together with others, some of whom they said were members of the Symbionese Liberation Army. One of my sources told me: "Our street sources tell us that the Manson-SLA group is planning something that will make the Patty Hearst thing look penny ante."

The FBI and police in several California cities put together this scenario:

- The Manson clan, some of whose members were convicted of the Tate-LaBianca murders, and the SLA had recruited new followers, and joined forces.
- The Manson-SLA group had gone on a crime spree that included a series of northern California bank robberies and an intricate and lucrative credit card scheme (that was Gypsy).
- According to the FBI, the group had raked in about $2 million, with the money to be used to free Charlie from prison. The group had also

stockpiled weapons and gold, and at least three of the group had learned to pilot helicopters.

But Charlie maintained he knew nothing of this. I don't know whether to believe him.

If it isn't clear from his own words, Charlie was a man who would have been more comfortable in another century. He believed women were there only for his comfort and he believed he had a divine right to control them. And, of course, wound through his talk of controlling women, he spoke of love and how important it was to him.

> We're accused of hypnotizing so they must be hypnotized watching their TVs and reading their newspapers. What happens when they all wake up? We're waking, and we see it as it was, as it's always been, as it will always be. My love is yours, yours in mine. You live inside of me. If my love is yours, then yours is mine. Give it all to yourself, for there is only one, and you are the one, the only one.
>
> Love places no meaning on anything. Only man has done that. Things are the way they are. Everything goes around, comes around. Mom and dad control your love's flow. Mother, then wife, an extension of mother. If a person loves his mom, he will do what his wife says. This often makes him her victim. If a mother loves her son, she will allow him to lead her, and make his own decisions and opinions, making him strong within himself. Mother was put here to take care of man, not to guide him, and pull him around by the hand. So many controls are put on children that it is hard to find a strong person who can stand alone with nothing the good in his heart.

He spoke often of control, his control of others, and the control of those who "passed judgment" on him and his Family.

> Fear is all the control anyone has over you. One can only be free when fear becomes love and awareness. In pure love, there is no fear—only

awareness. Be willing to experience fear. People fear what? The unknown? Pain? Starvation? Thirst in the desert? Drowning? If you are willing to completely experience anything your soul takes you through, then all the fear is gone and life really begins to move your love, and then you look face to face with your god. My god is love. You can get your own. Love is to me nothing—an endless void, contentment, peace, everything that moves, everything that does not move, them, those, yours, his, and above all, me. If I can't see his in me, then I can't see him in you. If you don't have the power in you, you'll never see but a mirror, a reflection of what you think you are seen through your eyes.

Turn off all outside opinions, for all the confusion has been put in our heads by the dead and the dying.

Even after the trial, the press wanted to talk to Charlie, and he often ran those requests by me. The London *Daily Mirror*'s U.S. bureau chief wrote to Charlie. Charlie was inclined to reject the request from *People* magazine, but he asked me what I thought. The *National Enquirer* sent a long letter offering a "generous" payment for the interview. They wanted to talk about Charlie's relationship with the Family, and what responsibility Presidents Nixon or Ford had in Charlie's conviction. Squeaky Fromme had just taken a potshot at President Ford, so they wanted to talk about that as well. Some of these he accepted, but the vast majority of the interviews he turned down. For the next forty years, journalists would trek to whichever prison Charlie was in to film documentaries, or relive the past in one form or another.

Charlie never stopped telling me that he was not guilty of the Tate-LaBianca killings. It is clear to me that he wasn't at either of the two houses at the time of the killings, but he was responsible. His control over the girls—Sadie, Leslie, Patricia—was absolute. The men were just as firmly under his thumb, men like Tex Watson, Bobby Beausoleil, or Bruce Davis, who said they would do anything for him, including murder. After the conviction, he spoke much more often of God than he did when in jail, or during trial:

> Saying you're sorry, or it wasn't me . . . I'm not the one who did all those things. . . . or God will help us. No, no, no, no, you won't be allowed to get away with it. God only sees one man and you are him. In God's eye, we are only one. No, you can't hide, only in love will you come to one with no fear in your heart, ready for the crosses again. In that valley of fear your love will be released to flow over the ether, cleaning and washing away the old and bringing the love back to where we were before words were learned, before the one was a one, the two can never exist in man's mind again.

In one of the last letters I still have from Charlie, he was clearly lonely. He had been asked to give multiple interviews, but the prison authorities told him he could only pick one, and he asked me to come see him. He wanted to get his words out to the wider world . . . a world that was still fascinated with him.

10 He Never Left the Public Eye

The public has never tired of reading about Charlie and his Family.

There have been movies, books, TV series, and more newspaper and magazine articles than can be counted. Each of the Family members was watched and written about endlessly. And the cult of Manson continued, with new followers every year.

One of those followers, a young woman named Afton Elaine Burton—but known as "Star"—moved to Corcoran in 2007 to be near Charlie. She visited him as often as she could for seven years, and the two were supposedly married in 2014. Charlie was eighty years old. Star was twenty-six. The press ate it up. The stories emphasized that Charlie was not eligible for conjugal visits. Charlie told one press outlet that it wasn't true, just made up for the press, but Star certainly acted as if it was a romance for the ages.

Of his original girls, many were either in prison or on parole: Gypsy Share, Squeaky Fromme, and others.

Sadie Atkins died in prison in 2009 from brain cancer.

With Sadie's death, Patricia Krenwinkel officially became the longest-serving female inmate in California history. She was denied parole more than fourteen times. She was granted parole in October 2022, but California's governor reversed the decision, saying she was still a danger to society.

After fifty years in prison, Leslie Van Houten was released on parole in 2023.

Bobby Beausoleil, Tex Watson, and Bruce Davis are still in prison as of this writing. Watson and Davis both "found God" in prison and became model prisoners.

Even the crime scene is gone—the Tate home was torn down in 1999, and an Italian-style mansion was erected in its place. The ramshackle structures that made up the Spahn Ranch burned down in 1970, and George Spahn died in 1974. Eventually, Spahn Ranch became part of a state park. The LaBianca home was sold in 2021 to Zak Bagans, the star of the Travel Channel's *Ghost Adventures,* but he soon sold it to someone else.

Every year, on the anniversary of the Tate-LaBianca killings, a story would appear. On the fortieth anniversary, a number of newspapers featured retrospectives on their front pages. The fiftieth anniversary saw interviews, articles, and podcasts. Charlie was, once again, front-page news. But he wasn't around to see that.

Charles Milles Manson died in prison on November 19, 2017, just a week after his eighty-third birthday. He left one son, Michael Brunner, the child of Mary Brunner, who was involved in the Gary Hinman killing. There may be others, but if there are, none have come forward. Michael Brunner is said to look a lot like Charlie did, but he is a private person, and he rarely talks to the press.

I wasn't comfortable talking about Charlie and me until after he died. So much of what he told me was "off the record," and I honored that. But I figured our agreement died with him. After all these years, reading his letters and revisiting all the articles I wrote about the trial has brought him alive again to me. The trial was a circus, as I said—and also some of the most rewarding times of my professional life.

Charlie knew he would never get out of prison through parole. He said that "they"—a word he used often—had turned him into a monster, and that everyone, including the parole board, was afraid of him. But he thought he might be able to escape. Before the Tate-LaBianca murders, he escaped from Terminal Island Prison in Los Angeles by manipulating the warden and a guard into making him a trustee. He walked out of the prison and was in the process of hot-wiring a car in the parking lot when the guards found him.

He thought he could do it again. Equipment like a guard's uniform, knives, keys, and more were found hidden in Charlie's cell. Charlie told me that guards left windows open—on purpose—hoping he would try to escape.

Too late now.

As for me, I'm almost the last man standing. Charlie is dead, as are most of the girls. Bugliosi died years ago, as did Judge Older. The defense is gone: Irving Kanarek, Paul Fitzgerald, Maxwell Keith. Most of the reporters are gone, too: Theo Wilson, Linda Deutsch, and so many others.

After the Manson trial, I went on to cover dozens of murder cases, some more gruesome than others. I dream things I should not dream. But I wouldn't change anything.

I had the best job in the world, the only job I ever wanted. I was a newspaper reporter.

Index

Alcatraz East Crime Museum, 122
Ambassador Hotel, 98, 109
animals, Manson connection to, 13–14, 108
Aryan Brotherhood, 59
Assassins . . . Serial Killers . . . Corrupt Cops: Chasing the News in a Skirt and High Heels (Neiswender), 62
Atkins, Sadie: background of, 23; Charlie Manson and, 3, 10, 24, 103; confession of, 86; conviction of, 78–79; courtroom antics of, 29, 30–31, 34, 101; criminal record of, 23–24; death of, in prison, 24, 30, 133; The Family and, 29–30, 126; Gary Hinman, murder of, 24, 56, 75; Sharon Tate, murder of, 31–32, 37, 62; Shorty Shea, murder of, 58; Tate-LaBianca murders and, 24, 41; testimony, coercion of, 10, 26, 31, 57; testimony, in exchange for leniency, 3, 23, 29, 101–2; testimony of, 7, 8, 24, 35, 104, 108. *See also* Charlie's girls; The Family
Atkins, Susan. *See* Atkins, Sadie

Ball, Joe, 79–80, 123
Barker Ranch, 47, 58–59
The Beach Boys, 5
The Beatles, 67, 103
Beausoleil, Bobby: Charlie Manson and, 130; Gary Hinman, murder of, 26, 56–58, 75, 86; Gypsy Share and, 41; Leslie Van Houten and, 35; trial of, 56–58. *See also* The Family
Bittaker, Lawrence, 37, 100
blood of victims, writing with, 34, 37, 55, 56, 57, 61, 62
Bonin, Bill (Freeway Killer), 7, 16, 37
Bonin, William. *See* Bonin, Bill (Freeway Killer)
Breckenridge, James: *Harvard Crimson* article and, 66, 68; Linda Kasabian and, 66–68; Manson trial, attendance of, 66
Brunner, Mary, 134; child with Manson, 43, 57, 134; Lynette "Squeaky" Fromme and, 33, 48; testimony of, 56, 57, 86
Brunner, Michael, 134
Bugliosi, Vince: Charlie Manson and, 111, 125; closing argument of, 106, 108; Danny DeCarlo, testimony of, 89; gag order, violation of, 108; "Helter Skelter" theory and, 67, 90, 102, 105; Irving Kanarek and, 85, 91, 100, 102–3, 106; Mary Neiswender and, 13, 68, 72, 99, 100; Maxwell Keith and, 27, 103; opening statement of, 94; opportunities, post-trial, 104; prosecution of, 24, 78, 88, 109; Sadie Atkins and, 24, 29, 30, 31, 101–2, 104; Terry Melcher, testimony of, 5; unprofessionalism of, 24, 72, 99–100, 101–3, 106, 108. *See also* Manson Trial
Burton, Afton Elaine, 133

Caballero, Richard, 102
Charles Manson Family. *See* The Family
Charlie's girls: abuse of, by Charlie Manson, 14–15, 26, 44, 49, 50, 121, 130; courthouse, presence outside, 8, 31, 35–36, 78, 113, 126; courtroom, antics of, 34, 78, 96; daily life of, at Spahn Ranch, 45–46; drug use and, 118; loyalty of, 8, 15, 25, 34–36, 40, 78, 91, 92, 108, 116, 121; press coverage of, 30; testimony, coercion of, 11, 81. *See also* The Family; Spahn Ranch
Chavez, Cesar, 21
Como, Kenneth: Charlie Manson, attack on, 124; Gypsy Share, marriage to, 124
copycat murders, 59–62
courthouse, outside, 8, 31, 35–36, 78, 113, 126
courtroom, inside, 9, 29, 30, 78, 84
cowboys of Spahn Ranch, interviews of, 49–50
credit card scam, 60–61, 124, 126, 128

Daily Mirror (London), 130
Davis, Angela, 21
Davis, Bruce, 8–9, 58, 130, 133
DeCarlo, Danny, 89
Dell, George, 80
DeLouise, Joseph: predictions made by, 73–75; threats made to, 75
Deutsch, Linda: Associated Press reporter, 64; Mary Neiswender, friendship with, 72; as "sob sister," 72
drugs, illicit, 27, 28, 31, 34, 35, 40, 79, 92, 101, 104, 105, 118

evidence, missed by investigators, 10

The Family: abuse of members, 14–15, 44, 49, 50, 121; album, independent release of, 6; Charlie Manson and, 117, 119, 126, 130; courthouse, presence outside, 8, 31, 35–36, 78, 113, 126; crimes committed by, 55, 61, 101, 128; Kenneth Como and, 124; loyalty of, 8, 15, 23, 35–36, 40, 48, 59, 60, 78, 83, 91, 92, 108, 116, 121; members, as witnesses, 11, 81–82; membership in, 47–49, 117, 133; murders, involvement in, 38; origination of, 42–43, 47, 50–51, 116–17; philosophy of, 47, 51, 52; public fascination with, 133; school bus used by, 48, 50–52; sex and, 13, 27, 44, 49, 89, 120; Shorty Shea, murder of and, 58; Symbionese Liberation Army (SLA) and, 128–29; testimony, coercion of, 56, 81; threats made by, 6, 68–69; threats made to, 11, 42, 81–82; *X*s, carving into foreheads, 8, 31, 59. *See also* Charlie's girls; Spahn Ranch
Fitzgerald, Paul: Linda Kasabian, testimony of, 28; Mary Neiswender, impression of, 66; mistrial motion, filing of, 106–7; Patricia Krenwinkel and, 31, 33. *See also* Manson Trial
Flynn, Juan, 49–50
Folger, Abigail, murder of, 28, 31, 34, 36, 78
Ford, Gerald, assassination attempt on, 16, 39, 126, 130
forensic technology, 58–59
"Free Charlie" fund, 61
Free Press (Los Angeles), 65
Freeway Killer. *See* Bonin, Bill (Freeway Killer)
Fromme, Lynette "Squeaky": Brenda McCann and, 42; Gerald Ford, assassination attempt on, 16, 39, 126, 130; Mary Neiswender, interview with, 39; testimony of, 48. *See also* Charlie's girls

Frykowski, Voytek, murder of, 28, 37, 78

Gibbons, Sandi: Charlie Manson, impression of, 126; City News Service (Los Angeles) and, 64; Mary Neiswender, friendship with, 72; as "sob sister," 72
Glutz, Sadie May. *See* Atkins, Sadie
Good, Sandra. *See* Good, Sandy
Good, Sandy: background of, 25; Bugliosi and, 101; conviction and exoneration of, 25; loyalty of, 25, 36, 126
Grogan, Steve "Clem," 58
Guatemala, earthquake of 1976, 22

Haight-Ashbury, 47, 48, 78
Harvard Crimson (Harvard University), 66, 68
"Helter Skelter" party: announcements for, 72; attendees, costumes of, 72; Charlie Manson and, 72; fallout from, 73; Vince Bugliosi and, 72
"Helter Skelter" theory, 13, 57–58, 67, 90–91, 94, 102, 103, 124
Hinman, Gary, murder of: Bobby Beausoleil and, 56, 57, 75; Charlie Manson and, 56, 86, 113, 122; The Family and, 25–26; Gypsy Share and, 41; Mary Brunner and, 56, 134; Sadie Atkins and, 54, 56, 57, 75
The Hippie Movement, 98–99; Charlie Manson and, 8, 15, 63, 68–69, 94, 105, 112; "Helter Skelter" party and, 72; Jeffrey MacDonald and, 62; Ron Hughes and, 88–89
Hitler, Adolph, 108
Hollopeter, Charles, 83
Hoyt, Barbara, 101
Hughes, Ronald: Charlie Manson and, 79; disappearance of, 84, 88–89; Leslie Van Houten and, 70, 86, 87; physical appearance of, 86–87. *See also* Manson Trial
Humboldt County, 60

Inyo County Courthouse, 93

journalism, women in, 2, 17
jury: alternate jurors, calling of, 112; deliberation of, 108–9; demographics of, 70; hardships of, 109, 112; influences on, 69–70; interviews of, post-trial, 109–10; press coverage of, 71; requests of, 103–4; security around, 108–9; selection of, 69–70, 84; transportation of, 109; verdict of, 78–79, 93, 109. *See also* Manson Trial

Kanarek, Irving: background of, 84; Charlie Manson and, 71, 85–86, 89–92, 94, 107, 111; closing argument of, 91, 104–6; Danny DeCarlo, cross-examination of, 89; Linda Kasabian, cross-examination of, 29; Vince Bugliosi and, 100, 101, 106. *See also* Manson, Charlie, defense of; Manson Trial
Kasabian, Linda: background of, 25; Bobby Beausoleil and, 26; child neglect and, 28, 68; drug use and, 27, 28; Gary Hinman murder and, 26, 41; immunity for testimony and, 3, 29; James Breckenridge and, 66–68; Spahn Ranch and, 26; Tate-LaBianca murders and, 25, 31–32; testimony of, 3, 8, 10, 27–29, 38, 66, 85, 102, 111. *See also* Charlie's girls; The Family
Kasindorf, Martin, 87
Kay, Steve: Gypsy Share and, 41; Sandy Good and, 101; Vince Bugliosi and, 100
Keene, William, 82–84, 95

Keith, Maxwell: Leslie Van Houten and, 89; Vince Bugliosi and, 103
Kennedy, Bobby, assassination of, 98
Kent State University shootings, 98
King County jailbreak, 60
Krenwinkel, Patricia, 7, 48, 130; background of, 25; Charlie Manson and, 33; conviction of, 25, 78–79; courtroom antics of, 34; drug use and, 34; The Family, joining, 33–34, 48; parole, denial of, 133; psychiatric evaluation of, 31–32; Tate-LaBianca murders and, 28, 33, 34, 103; testimony of, 34. *See also* Charlie's girls; The Family

LaBianca, Leno, murder of, 25, 27, 31, 34, 35, 37, 46, 78
LaBianca, Rosemary, murder of, 25, 27, 31, 34, 35, 37, 46, 78
LaBianca home: as crime scene, 4, 38, 103; sale of, 134
Levy, Robert, 83–84
Longshoreman's Union, 64
Los Angeles, downtown, description of, 8
Los Angeles County Jail, security restrictions of, 1, 3
Los Angeles Long Beach harbor, reporting from, 18–21
Los Angeles Police Department, mishandling of investigation and, 10
LSD use, 28, 34, 35, 40, 92, 101, 104, 105, 118
Lucas, Malcolm, 95

MacDonald, Grant, 20
MacDonald, Jeffrey: Charlie Manson, accusation of, 62; conviction of, 62; copycat killing and, 98; Mary Neiswender, interview of, 62; murder of family by, 61–62
Maddox, Cathleen, 16
Manson, Charles Milles. *See* Manson, Charlie
Manson, Charlie: Afton Elaine Burton and, 133; animals, connection to, 13–14, 108; background of, 2, 7, 16, 119; death of, in prison, 121, 134; education level of, 4; family history of, 16, 115; grandmother of, 16, 115, 119; institutions, time spent in, 118–19; mother of, 115, 119
Manson, Charlie, as cult leader: abuse of Family members and, 14–15, 44, 49, 50, 121; children, ideas about, 118, 129; as Christ figure, 9, 24, 39, 40, 50, 107, 112; demeanor of, 4, 14–15, 59, 80, 94, 118; drugs, approved by, 118; The Family and, 26, 47–48, 50–51, 116–17, 119, 120; "free love" and, 44, 121, 129; manipulation and, 8, 23, 49, 126–27, 129; philosophy of, 6, 13, 36, 51–53, 113, 117, 118, 123, 126–31; physical description of, 3, 7, 8, 69, 91–92, 103, 119; public fascination with, 3, 63, 64, 69, 133; women, view on, 129. *See also* Charlie's girls; The Family
Manson, Charlie, communication with Mary Neiswender: agreement between, 2, 13, 121, 134; boundary setting and, 15; communication, modes of, 15; communication between, 3, 6, 50–51, 115, 121, 122–25; establishing contact, by phone, 1–2; final visit, plan for, 121; first contact, face-to-face, 2–3, 4; as inside source, 15–16; interviews, exclusivity of, 3, 12, 65, 66–67, 75, 131; letters between, 112–13, 120–21, 122–24; relationship dynamics

of, 12, 15–16, 122; testimony, practicing of, 12; trust between, 69, 75; visiting procedure of, 3

Manson, Charlie, defense of: attorneys, court-appointed, 79, 95; denial of guilt, 4–5, 117, 118; law library, access to, 82; musical defense, proposal of, 3, 5, 7; press release, from jail, 112; pre-trial optimism, 4; privileges, revoking of, 77; self-representation and, 4, 70–71, 77, 80–82, 83, 90, 94–95, 104–5, 110, 112; strategy around, 3, 5, 7, 77, 81; testimony of, 107; witnesses for, 3, 4, 8, 11, 81–82. *See also* Kanarek, Irving; "pro per" representation

Manson, Charlie, musical aspirations of: album, independent release of, 6; audition, at Spahn Ranch, 5–6; as musician, 3, 5, 6, 11; record contract, denial of, 5; singing, in jail, denial of, 111

Manson, Charlie, prison sentence, post-trial: appeal, of sentence, 113, 130; attack, at Folsom Prison, 123; crimes, unrelated, and, 4, 5, 55, 56, 59–62; death of, in prison, 121, 134; death penalty, commuting of, 113; escaping from prison, thoughts on, 134; illness, in prison hospital, 121; letters, from admirers, 120–21, 122–25; loneliness during, 124–25, 131; the press and, 75–76, 130; prison life and, 115–16, 123–24; reflections during, 116; strip searches of, 120; treatment during, 82, 111, 120

Manson, William, 16

Manson-SLA group, theories around, 128–29

Manson Trial: Charlie Manson, outbursts of, 9, 29, 30, 34, 70–71, 78, 83, 84, 92, 96–97, 103, 107, 109, 110–111; Charlie Manson, physical changes of, 91–93; Charlie Manson, testimony of, 107; Charlie Manson and Judge Older, 97–98, 110–11; courthouse, scene outside, 8, 31, 35–36, 78, 113, 126; dress code during, 86–87; events surrounding, 98–99; jury release, during, 111–12; Los Angeles County Coroner, testimony of, 36–37; media coverage of, 8, 9, 24, 48–49, 63, 64, 65, 69, 71, 75–76, 82, 97, 112, 130, 134; media frenzy around, 63, 64, 69; Nazi salute, making of, 96–97; press, influence of, during, 73, 82, 87, 104; public fascination with, 3, 63, 64, 69, 133; verdict of, 36, 78–79, 93, 109. *See also* Bugliosi, Vince; Fitzgerald, Paul; Hughes, Ronald; jury; Kanarek, Irving; Manson, Charlie, defense of; Neiswender, Mary, Manson Trial and; Older, Charles; Stovitz, Aaron

Maxwell, Keith, 26–27, 89, 103

McCann, Brenda, 8; background of, 42; Charlie Manson and, 42; The Family, origin of, 42–43; Lynette "Squeaky" Fromme and, 42; Mary Neiswender, interview with, 42–46

media coverage, of Manson Trial, 9, 63, 64, 65, 69, 97, 130, 134

Melcher, Terry, 5; Charlie Manson and, 5–6; Tate killings, motive for, and, 57; testimony of, 5–6

Morehouse, Ruth Ann, 35–36

murder weapon, 10

music, using in Manson defense, 3, 5, 7

National Enquirer, 130

Nazi salute, making of, during Manson Trial, 96–97
Nazi swastika, carving into forehead, by Charlie Manson, 91–92
Neiswender, Mary, career of: awards and accolades of, 22, 64, 122; college years, 17; early years, 17–18; ethics of, 21, 66, 68; exclusive interviews of, 1–2, 21–22, 66; experience, as a woman, 2, 17–20, 63–64; Guatemala earthquake assignment, 22; Linda Deutsch, friendship with, 72; Los Angeles Long Beach harbor news beat assignment, 18–21; postwar Germany assignment, 21; *Press-Telegram* and, 18, 63, 65; Pulitzer Prize nominations, 122; reflections on, 1, 135; Sandi Gibbons, friendship with, 72; Theo Wilson, friendship with, 71–72
Neiswender, Mary, Manson Trial and: colorful language, using, 12–13, 15, 65–66; James Breckenridge and, 66–68; *Newsweek* article, 65; notes, subpoena for, 66; reflecting on, 134; reporting on, 48–49, 64, 65, 71, 73, 94; Ron Hughes and, 87–88; as "sob sister," 72; Spahn Ranch, visit to, 39–41, 43–46; threats and, 6, 68–69; Vince Bugliosi and, 13, 68, 72, 99, 100
Neiswender, Mary, reporting on Charlie Manson: death of Manson, reaction to, 121–22; description of Manson, in print, 15, 94; final visit to Manson, plan for, 121; interviewing Manson, reasons for, 16; interviews, exclusivity of, 3, 12, 65, 66–67, 75, 131; observations of, 6–7, 13; off the record agreement, 134; press, reaction to, 15, 16; relationship with Manson, 122
news industry: Manson Trial, coverage of, 9, 63, 64, 65, 69–70, 71, 97, 104, 130; wage gap in, 18; women, as journalists in, 2, 17–18, 64; women, depiction of, by, 71
Newsweek article, featuring Mary Neiswender, 65
Nixon, Pat, 21
Nixon, Richard and Manson Trial, 63, 79, 106, 107
Nixon White House, 98
Noguchi, Thomas, 36–37
nomadic lifestyle, Spahn Ranch and, 4
Norris, Roy, 100

Older, Charles, 29, 30, 34, 37, 85, 109; background of, 95; Charlie Manson and, 89–90, 96, 110–11; interview, refusal of, 99; as judge, 95, 96; jury release, during trial, 111–12; Patricia Krenwinkel and, 32–33; reputation of, 95; Vince Bugliosi and, 106. *See also* Manson Trial
orgies, Spahn Ranch and, 31, 49, 104

Parent, Steven, murder of, 38, 78
Pearl, Ruby, 47–48
People magazine, 130
Plumlee, Vernon, 59
Polanski, Roman, 5, 57
Poston, Brooks, 39
press corps: international news outlets of, 64–65; Manson Trial and, 9, 63, 64, 65, 69–70, 71, 97, 104, 130; women, as journalists in, 2, 17–18, 64; women, depiction of, by, 71
"pro per" representation, 77, 79, 80, 82, 90

race war theory, 57, 60, 67, 90, 102, 105
Reagan, Ronald, 95

record companies, 3, 5
Reiner, Ira, 86

San Pedro CA, 18–19, 21, 64
Schiller, Lawrence, 29–30
Scientology, 49–50
Scott, Colonel, 16
Scott, Darwin "Scotty," murder of, 5, 55
Sebring, Jay, murder of, 31, 37, 78
second-class citizens, women as, 18
Sexy Sadie. *See* Atkins, Sadie
Share, Katherine "Gypsy": background of, 41; credit card scam and, 60, 124, 126, 128; The Family and, 41; Kenneth Como, marriage to, 124; King County jailbreak and, 60; Mary Neiswender, interview with, 41, 44, 45, 46; Shorty Shea, murder of, 41; testimony of, 41–42. *See also* Charlie's girls; The Family
Shea, Shorty, murder of, 41, 49, 58, 113, 122
Sheely, Larry, 112
Shibley, George, 95
"silent majority," 98
SLA. *See* Symbionese Liberation Army (SLA)
"sob sisters," 72, 126
Spahn, George, 46, 134
Spahn Ranch, 41, 60; abuse on, 14–15, 44, 49, 50; animals and, 13; children living on, 43, 50; cowboys, interviews of, 49–50; daily life on, 31, 33, 45–46, 49, 91; description of, 11; drug use at, 28, 31, 118; "free love" at, 44, 47, 60; George Spahn and, 46, 134; "Gypsy Hut" on, 39, 40; Mary Neiswender, visit to, 39–41, 43–46; music and, 5–6, 45–46; orgies and, 31, 49, 104; residents of, 4, 23, 35, 89, 117; Sadie Atkins, testimony and, 29; Shorty Shea, murder of and, 58; as state park, 134; structures on, destroying of, 134
Starr, Randy, 6
Stovitz, Aaron: Irving Kanarek and, 85; Manson Trial, removal from, 100; Mary Neiswender, interview by, 99; Sadie Atkins testimony and, 31, 102; Universal Life Church and, 59. *See also* Manson Trial
strip searching, 82, 120
Symbionese Liberation Army (SLA): Charlie Manson and, 60–61; crimes connected to, 60–61; The Family and, 128–29

Tate, Debra, 59
Tate, Sharon, murder of, 1, 5, 7, 9–10, 24, 31–32, 37, 66, 78
Tate home: Charlie Manson visit to, 5; Mary Neiswender visit to, 9, 73; neighbor, interview of, 9–10, 66, 73; tearing down of, 134
Tate-LaBianca murders: Charlie Manson, involvement in, 7, 31–32, 103; evidence, recovery of, 10; motive for, 57; psychic predictions following, 73–75
telepathic communication, 126
The Killing of Sharon Tate (Schiller), 30
Tito, Josef, 21
Tribal Thumb, 60

Universal Life Church, 59
University of Southern California (USC): School of Journalism, 17–18

Van Houten, Leslie: background of, 25, 35; Bobby Beausoleil and, 35; conviction of, 25, 78–79; courtroom antics of, 34; drug use and, 35; The Family, joining, 35; La

Van Houten, Leslie (*continued*)
Bianca, Rosemary, murder of, and, 35; release of, 25, 133; Ronald Hughes and, 86–87; Tate-LaBianca murders and, 41; testimony of, 35. *See also* Charlie's girls; The Family
victims' blood, writing with, 34, 37, 55, 56, 57, 61, 62
Vietnam War, 98

wage gap, in the news industry, 18
Watson, Charles "Tex," 7, 28, 75, 130, 133; background of, 38; as "born-again" Christian, 39; LaBianca murder home and, 38; medically unfit for trial, 37–38; Shorty Shea, murder of, 58; Steven Parent, murder of, 38; Tate murder home, presence at, 38; Tate murders, involvement in, 31–32; trial of, 38–39. *See also* The Family
Watson, Chuck. *See* Watson, Charles "Tex"
Weiss, Steven, 10
White Album (Beatles), 103
Wilson, Dennis, 5
Wilson, Theo: *Daily News* (New York) reporter, 64, 65; Mary Neiswender, friendship with, 71–72; as "sob sister," 72
women, depiction of, in the media, 63–64
women, working in journalism, 64; prescribed roles for, 17; as second-class citizens, 18; wage gap and, 18

*X*s, carving into foreheads, 8, 31, 59

Younger, Evelle: gag order, violation of, 104; Irving Kanarek and, 85; press coverage and, 85, 104; Sadie Atkins, testimony of, 86, 102, 104; testimony of, 104

Zero, Christopher, 59